The Journal of the History of Philosophy Monograph Series
Edited by Richard H. Popkin and Richard A. Watson

Kant's Newtonian Revolution in Philosophy

By
Robert Hahn

Published for
The Journal of the History of Philosophy, Inc.

SOUTHERN ILLINOIS UNIVERSITY PRESS
Carbondale and Edwardsville

Copyright © 1988 by
The Journal of the History of Philosophy, Inc.
All rights reserved
Printed in the United States of America
Designed by Cindy Small
Production supervised by Linda Jorgensen-Buhman

91 90 89 88   4 3 2 1

Library of Congress Cataloging-in-Publication Data

Hahn, Robert, 1952–
Kant's Newtonian revolution in philosophy
by Robert Hahn
p. cm.—(Journal of the history of philosophy monograph series)
"Published for the Journal of the history of philosophy, Inc."
Bibliography: p.
ISBN 0-8093-1441-X (pbk.)
1. Kant, Immanuel, 1724–1804. Kritik der reinen Vernunft.
2. Kant, Immanuel, 1724–1804—Contributions in scientific method.
3. Newton, Isaac, Sir, 1642–1727—Contributions in scientific method.
I. Title. II. Series.
B2779.H34   1988
121'.092'4—dc19   87-17618   CIP

The paper in this publication meets the minimum requirements of
American National Standard for Information Sciences—Permanence of
Paper for Printed Library Materials, ANSI Z39.48-1984. ∞™

For my parents

CONTENTS

Chapter 7
Rethinking the Revolutionary Contributions
of Copernicus and Galileo to the
Natural Science That Kant Understood
74

7.A. The Revolutionary Consequences of Copernicus'
Hypothesis: Toward a Transformation in
the Traditional Disciplinary Matrix
74

7.B. Aristotle, Galileo, and Kant: Toward a
Transformation in the Logic of Demonstration
82

Chapter 8
Kant's Copernican Hypothesis:
Science, Metaphysics, and the Pursuit
of Synthetic a priori Judgments
88

8.A. Kant's Novel Hypothesis
88

8.B. Was Kant's Novel Hypothesis about the
Foundation of Certain Knowledge Revolutionary?
89

Chapter 9
Kant's Newtonian Revolution:
Transcendental Arguments and the Requirement
of Demonstration in the *Critique*
101

9.A. Kant's Problem of Demonstration in General
101

9.B. Demonstration *Quid Facti* and the
Irrational Knowledge of the Rational
103

THE *JOURNAL OF THE HISTORY OF PHILOSOPHY*
Monograph Series

THE *JOURNAL OF THE HISTORY OF PHILOSOPHY* MONOGRAPH SERIES, consisting of volumes of 80 to 120 pages, accommodates serious studies in the history of philosophy that are between article length and standard book size. Editors of learned journals have usually been able to publish such studies only by truncating them or by publishing them in sections. In this series, the *Journal of the History of Philosophy* presents, in volumes published by Southern Illinois University Press, such works in their entirety.

The historical range of the *Journal of the History of Philosophy* Monograph Series is the same as that of the *Journal* itself – from ancient Greek philosophy to the twentieth century. The series includes extended studies on given philosophers, ideas, and concepts; analyses of texts and controversies; new translations and commentaries on them; and new documentary findings about various thinkers and events in the history of philosophy.

The editors of the Monograph Series, the directors of the *Journal of the History of Philosophy,* and other qualified scholars evaluate submitted manuscripts.

We believe that a series of studies of this size and format fulfills a genuine need of scholars in the history of philosophy.

Richard H. Popkin
Richard A. Watson
– Editors

Kant's Newtonian Revolution
in Philosophy

CHAPTER 1

Introduction

THE REVOLUTION IN PHILOSOPHY THAT KANT PROPOSES TO EFFECT IN THE *Critique of Pure Reason*, as announced in the B Preface of 1787, is a Newtonian, or even Keplerian, but not a Copernican revolution.[1] The commonplace that Kant effects a Copernican revolution in philosophy misrepresents Kant's expressed statements on the matter, it distorts Kant's view of Copernicus, and it misleads us in our effort to understand what the scientific revolution—the revolution in natural science or physics—meant to him. Thus, to object to the claim that Kant effects a Copernican revolution is no mere quibble about an expression. To comprehend that Kant believes himself to be effecting a Newtonian revolution is to come to terms with the specific model on whose analogy Kant constructs his own critical philosophy, and hence the importance of the specific character of the scientific revolution as he understood it.

Such a reconsideration is all the more significant given recent work in the history of science that has called into serious question the very idea that a scientific revolution took place at all—that "revolution" properly describes the emergence and growth of scientific knowledge. Since Kant's influence, especially through the *Critique*, has been very great in the last century and a half, problems inherent in supposing that a revolution took place in science, can be traced back to Kant. A major objective of this essay is to unmask the Kantian origins of our contemporary thought of a scientific revolution.

Kant's Newtonian revolution in philosophy attempts to reveal the method or procedure of science, for it is expressly in terms of that model that Kant constructs his critique of traditional metaphysics. Accordingly, the first task of this Introduction, in section 1.A, is to examine the structure of that method. When that is accomplished, our path away from Copernicus and toward Newton will be cleared for a deeper examination. Second, in section 1.B, once that structure has been isolated, the plan of the first *Critique* presents itself as both a science and a purported

1

2 • KANT'S NEWTONIAN REVOLUTION

revolution overthrowing traditional philosophy—dogmatic and sceptical, rationalist and empiricist—and the relation of that enterprise to recent work in metaphysics and epistemology requires a brief consideration. Here, I wish to suggest what is inadequate about Kant's purported revolution as a solution to traditional metaphysics, and the task that still lies before us. In a phrase, Kant's project in philosophy hinges on his understanding of the scientific revolution. This essay will suggest that what is mistaken in his critical and theoretical philosophy is the very same error that he made in assessing the idea of a scientific revolution: there is no more a privileged or God's eye point of view of subjectivity than there is an objective knowledge of the thing-in-itself. In denying (1) certain knowledge of the object, independent of our conscious states, Kant believed that he had not abandoned a vision of objective and certain knowledge, by (2) supposing that he could save a meaning of objectivity by revealing the a priori structure of subjectivity. The task of philosophy now, as I see it, seems to be to grant Kant's objection to (1), deny him (2), and then determine how it is yet possible to save a meaningful sense of objectivity. This is the project of internal realism, to use Hillary Putnam's locution. The problem is to deny a God's eye point of view— in the object or subject—without reducing thought to "Anything goes." Then, thirdly, in section 1.C, I indicate a leading edge in the history and philosophy of science that has called into question the very idea that a scientific revolution took place at all, that the expression revolution is perhaps both misleading and inappropriate to account for the historical enterprises in the growth and development of science. Finally, in the last section of this Introduction, section 1.D, the plan of this monograph is announced in nine chapters.

1.A. Kant and the Structure of Scientific Method

Kant envisages his *Critique* on the order of Newton's *Principia*, and following the method detailed in his *Opticks*, even more so than the geometry compiled and perfected by Euclid. For unlike mathematics, natural science found its way onto the secure road to certainty, employing the hypothetico-deductive method, and philosophy, in Kant's view, ought to follow that method. The method in natural science differs from mathematics because philosophy, like physics, must deal with given empirical objects. In mathematics, on the contrary, Reason deals with itself alone. Consequently, philosophy ought not employ the method of mathematics. It should rather try to imitate, in Kant's estimation, the method in the natural sciences. The method of demonstration in the sciences has two distinct moments: (1) a novel hypothesis, and (2) a rigorous deduction. The rigorous deduction is the focus of Kant's concern for through it objectivity in knowledge is established. The hypothesis, although indispensable to the successful deduction, is incapable, by itself, of securing that essential objectivity.

In Kantian terms, Copernicus represents the formulator of a novel hypothesis, while Newton represents the provider of a rigorous deduction. Thus, to identify Kant's contribution with a Copernican revolution, in his own terms, would be to cast him into the role of a mere formulator of hypotheses, and not the provider of a rigorous deduction—a role that he explicitly rejects. To suppose that Kant seeks to achieve a revolution on the order that he judged to have been effected by Copernicus is to misunderstand what Copernicus meant to Kant, what scientific revolution meant and how it was effected. For it is on that model of a scientific revolution that he fashions his revolution for metaphysics. This essay advances the thesis that Kant believed himself to be effecting a Newtonian revolution in philosophy, a revolution on the order of Newton's *Principia*, the rigorous deduction of universal gravitation, and hence justification of the general laws of motion. Kant did not envision the *Critique* as merely the instrument for promulgating an unproven heliocentric hypothesis. To understand the difference we must investigate what counted as a demonstration for Kant, why Newton provides one in Kant's estimation while he denies it to Copernicus, and how the revolution that Kant effects in metaphysics depends upon a new meaning of demonstration.

Kant defines a new method of demonstration as a consequence of rejecting the deductive methods of a Cartesian or rationalist system, on the one hand, and by denying the legitimacy of the inductive methods of the empiricists like Hume and Locke, on the other. Rejecting rationalist procedure, Kant claims that the establishment of principles cannot be secured by an ultimate appeal to mere self-evidence. Denying the empiricist's purported proof, he argues also that principles cannot be secured by induction from experience. Kant's task was to formulate, on analogy with the natural sciences as he understood them, how principles may be arrived at if one simultaneously rejects both methods as unsatisfactory. The empiricist program cannot yield the essential requirement of knowledge with certainty; the rationalist program offers certainty at the price of admitting the wild and ridiculous. Kant's new method of demonstration, imitating what he supposed was the method of the sciences, offered the prospect of a certainty whose validity, curiously enough, depended upon its application to (possible) experience. This strategy requires that we rethink the meaning of certainty, for it can no longer represent that absolute that the rationalists sought, and the empiricists rejected. The certainty Kant pursues was too weak for the rationalist programs, and too strong for that of the empiricists.

By rejecting the rationalist strategy, Kant rejects the reductionist program. The power of that project consisted in an ultimate appeal to self-evident principles, established by an appeal to logic: the law of noncontradiction. This was the heart of objectivity for the rationalists. When Kant turns away from that enterprise he is saddled with the difficulty of justifying his principles. He thus must find an ultimate ground for his principles (i.e., objectivity), which nonetheless is, in this sense, non-logical. This is a consequence of granting Hume's discovery of the synthetic character of the principle of causality. Indeed, it is an expression of Kant's recognition that since the principles of knowledge are ultimately synthetical, the intrinsic necessity claimed for principles by the rationalists is unacceptable.

Kant's denial of the empiricist strategy consists in his peculiar embrace of the a priori, and thus the demand for certainty, a demand that induction could never fulfill. The strong empiricist program amounts to a confession of scepticism: knowledge (equals certainty) is impossible; at best, our knowledge is probable. The a priori element that Kant seeks to secure is the universal and necessary structure of experience—its form—and in that consists his claim to have discovered the objective ground of knowledge. And yet, forsaking the reductionist/rationalist programs, the certainty that these a priori structures make possible is a peculiarly relative sort of certainty. This is because the proof of these a priori structures is neither inductive (i.e., empirical), nor logical as if deduced from some absolutely necessary structure of thought itself.

Kant understands these a priori structures to be fundamentally relational. No mere analysis of the synthetical character of principles could alone reveal their objective ground. As a consequence, he advances a new method of demonstration that he comes to call transcendental proof: granting the fact that we do have experience, Kant attempts to isolate the conditions that must be presupposed to have that experience at all. Hence, the principles he secures are relative to—and thus valid for —possible experience only, and thus can have no absolute necessity or certainty. The universal and necessary forms of thought are conditional in just this sense. This peculiarly conditional dimension of universality and necessity is Kant's strategy for attaining objectivity in knowledge. Kant's transcendental idealism is at once a sure commitment to empirical realism: he wants to embrace the rationalist's search for certainty while rejecting both the reductionist program and the specific content of the assertions secured by that ill-fated project; he wants to accept the empiricist's experimental efforts—trial and error—while denying the scepticism that he regarded as an inescapable consequence of the empiricist's program.

Unlike the tradition that preceded him, whose source was no less than Aristotle, which insisted that principles were neither in need of nor indeed capable of demonstration, Kant's project is to show that principles are both in need of and capable of proof. This new method and strategy of demonstration takes as its point of departure the supposition—the hypothesis—that the principles are both synthetical and a priori. The so-called factual statements of science cannot be secured apart from the principles, and the principles cannot be established apart from those claims. The demonstration of a principle consists in its adequacy to the interpretation of those appearances that it illuminates, while the demonstration of an asserted fact, that is, of our description of a given appearance, consists in its conformity to the principles that account for its very possibility.

Kant's theory of demonstration is another way of characterizing his vision of a coherence theory of truth. The validity of a theoretical principle for Kant consists in its adequacy to harmonize appearances, by revealing the conditions of their possibility. Its necessity is extrinsic, for their validity rests upon the presumption of a human, sensible experience alone, and thus are valid only *ex hypothesi*. This is Kant's transcendental method. The transcendental method—and transcendental argument—is his new procedure of demonstration. And this new method of demonstration shares precisely the same character that Kant believes is employed in the natural sciences, the hypothetico-deductive method. That method in the sciences begins with a phenomenon to be accounted for, and proceeds to determine—granting the appearance—the conditions that must be fulfilled in order to account for that given experience. Beginning with the given, the principles that account for its possibility are sought; in turn, those principles have a validity but only for those given appearances. At the close of his *Opticks*—a book which Kant owned[2]—Newton describes just this scientific method, in terms of analysis and synthesis, in just this fashion, and it is this methodology that Kant explicitly adopts and seeks to imitate. It is explicitly in terms of this model that Kant proceeds to construct his critique of pure reason. The following passage from Newton's *Opticks* is divided into two parts to emphasize this method. The first part characterizes the hypothetical method, the second the deductive method. Together they constitute the theory of demonstration.

[The method of hypothesis:] As in mathematics, so in natural philosophy, the investigation of difficult things by the method of analysis, ought ever to precede the method of composition. This analysis consists in making experiments and observations, and in drawing general conclusions from them by induction. . . . By this way of analysis we may proceed from compounds to ingredients, and from motions to the forces producing them; and in general from the effects to their causes, and from particular causes to more general ones, til the argument end in the most general. This is the method of analysis:[3]

[The method of deduction:] and the synthesis consists in assuming the causes discover'd and establish'd as principles, and by them explaining the phenomena proceeding from them and proving the explanations.[4]

This passage from the *Opticks* suggests quite clearly that analysis and synthesis (or composition), for Newton, meant induction and deduction.[5] Kant envisages this combination as the proper mediation between the inductive strategies of the empiricists and the deductive strategies of the rationalists. Neither method alone was adequate. Kant's method of demonstration seeks to imitate the hypothetico-deductive method employed by natural science, so clearly articulated by Newton; both enterprises, in Kant's estimation, rely on an indispensable commitment to a coherence theory of truth.

In the method of analysis, a method of induction is employed advancing more and more general hypotheses in the attempt to account for multifarious phenomena. The most general hypotheses arrived at will be the ultimate principles of those phenomena. At this point, however, the method of analysis has succeeded only in securing the most general principles hypothetically, through inductive generalization. The principles thus have a merely conditional necessity. Without the method of synthesis—the rigorous deduction—there is, at this point, no way to distinquish the hypothesis under consideration from the wild and ridiculous ones that have characterized metaphysical speculation at the time of Kant's writing, and have cast the "Queen of all the sciences" into such ridicule.

In the method of synthesis, a method of deduction is employed in which the phenomena under consideration are shown to be consequences that follow directly from these principles. The principles are thus shown to be adequate to the phenomena by exhibiting the conditions without which the phenomena themselves would not be possible. And when, the most general hypothesis arrived at by the method of analysis that has a merely conditional necessity—and hence is called an hypothesis—is exhibited to be the condition without which certain phenomena would not be possible, that hypothetical principle has bestowed upon it an unconditional or absolute necessity, thus properly entitling it to be called a principle. Kant's method of demonstration thus imitates the hypothetico-deductive method of the natural sciences; both suppose a coherence theory of truth.

1.B. Kant's Revolution Was an Inadequate Metaphysical Solution

In *Reason, Truth, and History*, Hillary Putnam sums up Kant's theory of knowledge as follows: "Truth is ultimate goodness of fit."[6] This is another way of stating that Kant is the proponent of a coherence theory of truth. What Putnam realizes is that Kant led the way toward our contemporary discussions of internal realism by rejecting the project of traditional philosophy. That project, broadly speaking, was directed toward grasping the essential nature of the real, which was supposed to be inherent in things, independent of the contents of our consciousness. In a word, this was the traditional search for the thing-in-itself. That project was made possible by accepting the commonsense presupposition that the contents of our consciousness must somehow correspond to the objects outside of and external to that consciousness that somehow cause us to have those specific representations that we in fact have: the similitude theory of reference.

On Putnam's account, Kant abandons the similitude theory of reference, by denying that our mental representations correspond, and thus are thus similar to, those things outside and independent of our consciousness, which are somehow the source of those representations. While it is true that Kant himself argues for a privileged point of view—now in terms of the a priori structure of thought—Kant denies the possibility, and thus the entire program, of a privileged and traditional external realism. If our mental representations—the contents of consciousness—cannot be mapped onto the things which are represented, because our knowledge of objects must always conform to the a priori structures of thought which we impose upon the contents of sensation, then to what do our specific representations refer? There is no one-to-correspondence between things-for-us and things-in-themselves. Thus Kant denies a correspondence theory of truth; the truth of a claim rests on a coherence theory—truth is ultimate goodness of fit. " 'Truth' in any other sense is inaccessible to us and inconceivable by us."[7]

When Thomas Kuhn wrote the *Structure of Scientific Revolutions,*[8] according to Putnam, he went too far in setting out a theory that knowledge is context dependent. If the growth of knowledge consists in radical revolutions that entirely revise the context in which statements are assessed, then Kuhn cannot escape the infelicitous charge of contextual relativism—which, for Putnam, amounts to the unacceptable declaration that "Anything goes." If knowledge is always within a context, and that context is historically determined, and thus to a degree entirely inaccessible to persons outside of that context, then there can be no objectivity in knowledge. Proponents of internal realism, like Putnam, and like Kant, want to rescue knowledge from mere scepticism. And if that charge is to be fulfilled, some sense of objectivity must be preserved. Otherwise, as Putnam so bluntly put it, we are saddled with " . . . a facile relativism that says, 'Anything goes.' "[9]

When Kant envisages a scientific revolution to have occurred, he grants—as does Kuhn—the discontinuous growth of knowledge. But, unlike Kuhn, Kant finds himself satisfied to affirm a privileged point of view that rescues knowledge from just this sort of facile relativism. This is because revolution, for Kant, although connoting discontinuity, also denoted a definitive stage that ultimately established knowledge with certainty. The certainty was achieved through the realization of the a priori foundation of knowledge that characterized those enterprises deserving to be called science, and opened up a domain that Kant could regard as objective. When Kuhn thinks of revolution, his historical investigations convince him that there is no royal road to certainty, and thus no objectivity of the sort Kant believed he had discovered. In Kantian terms, it might be fair to say that Kuhn, in the *Structure of Scientific Revolutions,* succumbs to the strong empiricist program that leads inevitably and unacceptably to scepticism.

The program of Kant's *Critique of Pure Reason*, and Kuhn's 1962 position in the *Structure of Scientific Revolutions* were both inadequate. Although both bought the thesis that knowledge is context-dependent, both did so at different but unacceptable prices. Kant insisted that there was a privileged perspective from which to assess all contexts; the exorbitant price he pays for objectivity is a pie-in-the-sky account of a priori subjectivity. Kuhn insisted, on the contrary, that there was no privileged frame of reference; the price of his own argument forced the sale of a meaningful sense of objectivity. Kant bought the rights to objectivity at too high a price; Kuhn sold the rights to objectivity for a trifle.

Along the same lines, although both Kant and Kuhn have employed the term "revolution," they have done so in different ways; their use of the term is equivocal. Kant's proposes to effect a revolution in metaphysics, and epistemology. His critique rests upon two presuppositions of the structure of the revolution that he believed was effected by natural science: (a) a coherence theory of truth, together with (b) a concept of objectivity that made certainty—and hence a privileged point of view—possible. In his 1962 work, Kuhn generally accepts (a) while rejecting (b).

However ingenious was the idea to maintain (a) a coherence theory of truth, alongside (b) an insistence upon the possibility of an objectivity grounded in the a priori, Kant's project could not succeed. Despite the exceptional clarity that he brought to the central problem of metaphysics, he too was a victim of his own historical context, and from which—despite his insistence to the contrary—he could not extricate himself, and thus rise above. The admission, following those like Kuhn and Quine, that knowledge is context-dependent, together with the aspiration to avoid a facile relativism and rescue some suitable meaning for objectivity, is the task that lies before contemporary discussions in the history and philosophy of science, in metaphysics and epistemology. The bulk of this essay is devoted to the far more modest challenge of flushing out the historical context, replete with ambiguities, of Kant's vision.

1.C. Rethinking Kant's Vision of a Scientific Revolution: Did a Revolution in Science Take Place at All?

Even physics, therefore, owes the beneficent revolution in its point of view entirely to the happy thought, that while reason must seek in nature, not fictitiously to ascribe to it, whatever as being not knowable through reason's own resources has to be learnt, if learnt at all, only from nature, it must adopt as its guide, in so seeking, that which it has itself put into nature. It is thus that the study of nature has entered on the secure path of a science. [Bxiv] . . . The examples of mathematics and natural science, which by a single and sudden revolution have become what they are now, seem to me sufficiently remarkable to suggest our considering what may have been the essential features in the changed point of view by which they have so greatly benefitted. Their success should incline us, at least by way of experiment to *imitate* their procedure. . . . We should then be proceeding precisely on the lines of Copernicus' primary hypothesis. [Bxvi][10]

Kant's *Critique of Pure Reason* can be viewed as both a philosophical interpretation of the scientific revolution he believed was effected, and as an illustration of a scientific method that he believed enabled various human enterprises to enter onto the "sure path of a science." In this fashion, Kant's *Critique* is an experiment, whose hypothesis exhibits a transformation in point of view indispensable for a scientific revolution, and whose demonstration is not only the definitive mark of a revolutionary achievement (hence, a scientific revolution) but also shows how far that scientific method may be successfully applied to metaphysics. Following Kant's discovery of what he claims to have been discovered by students of natural science, he attempts to demonstrate that metaphysics too can be guided onto the sure path of a science. In order to understand the difficulties inherent in such a view, I turn briefly to consider the current challenge to the very idea that a scientific revolution occurred at all.

The expression "scientific revolution" has become familiar in two related contexts. First, it has been used by those like Thomas Kuhn, in *The Structure of Scientific Revolutions*, to describe a "transformation in point of view" or "paradigm" that, by shaking the practice of science from its previously established roots, forces a reassessment of and redirection in the goals of the enterprise and research programs that pursue them, which in turn forces one to reinterpret the parts and practices of the normal science of puzzle-solving, which operate within a certain point of view or paradigm. The expression "scientific revolution" thus calls into question the idea of a cumulative nature of the scientific enterprise—and thus the growth of knowledge in general—since by dislodging the practice from its earlier roots, and grounding it within a new context, scientific revolutions are supposed to force a radical reorganization of a discipline.[11] The expression is also familiar in the form "the scientific revolution," as in the title of A. Rupert Hall's *The Scientific Revolution: 1500–1800*, which claims to isolate an historical period in which a decisive chapter of human enterprise unfolds.[12] Central aspects of both of these familiar senses of the expression "scientific revolution" are to be found in Kant's conception of it.

Expressions like "revolution," scientific or otherwise, are useful when they draw our attention to radical upheavals, real or imagined. But, further historical investigations, when they demonstrate the difficulty of precisely describing what upheavals if any are at issue, how, when, and if, they started, and exactly what the transition envisaged actually is, have the effect of undermining the very usefulness of such expressions. "Revolution" becomes not merely overworked but rather misleading when the events which it is designed to illuminate cast more question upon the appropriateness of the parlance than an intelligible vision through its employment. If the expression "scientific revolution" finds application to those like Copernicus,[13] then we are called to wonder about the appropriateness of the expression when we discover that among his contemporaries, his work did not seem to have any such immediate effect, as the battles of Lexington and Concord ushered in the American Revolution or the storming of the Bastille announced unmistakably the French Revolution. It took seventy-three years from the date of publication of Copernicus' *De Revolutionibus* until it appeared in the Catholic Index of Prohibited Books, and almost a century from its publication until the trial in which Galileo was condemned for teaching, holding, and defending the Copernican theory.[14]

Now, if it should be insisted that, despite Copernicus' own sense of his achievement, or the assessment by his contemporaries, from our current vantage point he indeed effected a revolution, it would still not be clear that the use of such parlance was instructive or appropriate. For revolutions—if we follow Kuhn's instruction—undermine the cumulative vision of the scientific enterprise, offer no good argument for a privileged position of assessment, no God's eye point of view from which we could present an ultimate papal decree on the nature of true insight.[15] Precisely because Kuhn does not permit truth to be a criterion of scientific theories, the usefulness of applying the expression "revolution" to historical achievements not viewed as revolutionary within their own immediate contexts is at best questionable.

When it becomes increasingly difficult to demonstrate just where and when revolutions began and transpired, the usefulness of such an expression naturally falls into doubt, and the appropriateness of freely employing locutions such as the "scientific revolution" seems equally suspicious without the clear-cut transitions that the expression currently suggests. It might prove to be felicitous to reexamine the use of expressions like "scientific revolution" in the attempt to illuminate various chapters in human intellectual development. In this essay, I shall confine myself to an examination of the use of this parlance by the influential Kant, who finds it useful, preoccupied with the very idea of revolutions in thinking, in the *Critique of Pure Reason*, to envisage his revolutionary contribution to philosophy on some sort of analogy with the growth and development of natural science. Inspired by efforts real or imagined, undertaken by those like Bacon, Galileo, Torricelli, and Stahl, Kant sets out to accomplish for metaphysics what he believes others have accomplished, for the natural sciences, by effecting a "revolution in thinking," a *Revolution der Denkart*.

Unmistakably, Kant is taken by what he perceives to be an enormous and rapid advance in natural science, and tries to account for its success. At the same time, metaphysics has grown farther away from natural science, and for him that means farther into ridicule. The natural sciences were supposed to provide satisfactory answers to vexing questions about reality broadly conceived. Kant wonders whether he can set metaphysics onto the secure path of a science, as have these other enterprises, entered by a "sudden revolution" (Bxvi) in thought.

The case has been made eloquently by Stegmüller,[16] Buchdahl,[17] and Brittan,[18] that Kant's *Critique* can be seen as a philosophical justification of Newton's *Principia*. Kant envisages Hume's attack on the validity of causal inference as an attack on the possibility of all empirical knowledge.[19] Kant's argument against Hume thus becomes *ex hypothesi* an argument for the validity of Newtonian physics. Kant seeks to show that Newton's claims ultimately rest upon unquestionable premises about the very fact of consciousness, and thereby the very possibility of having an experience. The validity of Newton's physics is thus seen as a consequence of Kant's metaphysics, which establishes this fact of consciousness in the context of articulating a theory, which Strawson succinctly described, about the necessary conditions for having any experience whatever.[20] Since Kant understands Copernicus to have introduced a novel hypothesis that gained established certainty from Newton's demonstration of the laws of motion (Bxxii, note), a formulation which Kant insists that Newton would never have discovered without Copernicus, then the revolutionary status of Kant, as he himself imagines it, is not merely placed alongside that of others like Newton, but rather underlies and supersedes their revolutionary achievements, while joining their ranks at the same time. Thus, this much seems clear from the outset: Kant supposes that various human enterprises entered onto an infallible path by a certain revolution in thinking, and Kant is convinced that he has achieved a comparable revolution in philosophy—for metaphysics—by discovering their fundamental insight, and by demonstrating the foundation of their own achievements. To realize this goal, Kant proposes, in the B Preface, an *Experiment der reinen Vernunft* (Bxxi, note) an "experiment of pure reason." He goes so far as to say that this experiment admits of "confirmation" or "refutation" modeled upon the method of the students of nature (Bxix, note). He introduces his claim as a novel hypothesis, along the lines of the first thought of Copernicus, and insists that the rigorous deduction, the apodeictic proof, is constituted by the *Critique* itself. That apodeictic proof is Kant's Newtonian revolution in philosophy.

Thus, Kant's appraisal of his own project proves to be an appraisal of revolutions in thinking—specifically, the revolution in science. From this point of view, the *Critique of Pure Reason* offers us an eighteenth-century enlightenment assessment of the so-called scientific revolution from a thinker who perceived himself, not so much in the midst of one, as at the outcome of one, whose successful principles he hoped to employ for the comparable revolution he proposed to effect for metaphysics. Whatever the scientific revolution meant to Kant he gave expression to in formulating the argument structure of the *Critique*, for it was only by isolating the fundamental ingredient of its methodological success as a science that, in following its successful employment, he would demonstrate the science of metaphysics.

1.D. The Plan of This Essay

Kant's enterprise in the *Critique of Pure Reason* is to attempt to place metaphysics on *der sichere Gang einer Wissenschaft*, on "the secure path of a science," convinced that other enterprises like logic, mathematics, and natural science, have achieved their success by securing such a path.[21] Entering onto this royal road, for Kant, is the result of an experiment, the designs of which he believes he has discovered, and which he makes "trial" of, in the *Critique*. The general structure of that experiment has two main features, following the hypothetico-deductive model he indeed recognizes and embraces: (1) the introduction of a novel hypothesis, and (2) a demonstration of that hypothesis that transforms the merely hypothetical into established certainty.

In the B Preface to the *Critique*, Kant envisages his enterprise, on the one hand, by analogy with Copernicus, who introduced a novel and indispensable hypothesis, and whose established certainty, on the other hand, was provided by Newton's (and Kepler's) laws of motion. The scholarly literature on Kant has spoken unclearly about this analogy, but has termed the scope of the Kantian enterprise a Copernican revolution in philosophy. By investigating and clarifying the analogy, greater insight into Kant's project, and Kant's understanding of the so-called scientific revolution is sought.

To reach this clarification, Chapter 2 provides a thorough if not exhaustive examination of Kant's use of the term "revolution" focusing upon the relevant uses in the *Critique of Pure Reason*, but also surveying both earlier and later occurrences of this technical parlance. Then, in Chapter 3, I examine the philosophical implications of Kant's use of revolution in the B Preface of the *Critique*, on the analogy with the revolution in natural science, in order to clarify the scope of his project. The structure of the science on which he models his metaphysics is examined in terms of the concept of experiment; serious question is raised about the historical arguments advanced both in the case of the early Greek mathematicians and the students of nature such as Galileo, Torricelli, and Stahl. I argue that a review of the historical dimensions of Kant's claims undermine the argument he proposes. In Chapter 4, I survey the identification of Kant's critical thought with the so-called Copernican revolution in the extensive array of scholarly literature in order to emphasize not merely how entirely widespread and well entrenched is this ill-begotten view, but also the serious defects expressed in this analogy. A chief objective is to make clear that Copernicus represents for Kant an illustrious case of the hypothetical moment in the scientific hypothetico-deductive method. Since the rigorous deduction becomes identified, for Kant, with the definitive mark of an intellectual revolution, and Kant believes he has effected one, Kant could not have envisioned his contribution on the order he judged appropriate to Copernicus' contribution. In Chapter 5, granting the results of the preceding chapter, I then flush out the relevant meanings and ambiguities of "hypothesis" as they bear directly on Kant's understanding of Copernicus and his contribution to the methodology of the critical project. Thus, Kant's self-proclaimed revolution is contrasted with his view of hypotheses and their place in this revolution. The intention is to clarify further why it is misleading to erroneously credit Kant with effecting a Copernican revolution in philosophy.

In Chapter 6, the historical context of Kant's ideology is explored. Having explicated the few references Kant makes to Copernicus, I clarify just what it is that Kant does say and the context in which he says it. I then turn to consider the source from which I have come to suppose that Kant indeed learned his Copernicus. I argue that it seems unlikely that Kant ever read *De Revolutionibus*, and that in any case when he writes the B Preface it seems likely that he is thinking of an account with which he was surely familiar since at least 1759 and 1760, when he taught courses in mechanics, and probably much earlier, from Wolff's *Elementa Matheseos Universae*. To make the case, I present relevant quotations from Wolff's treatise on scientific method—the "Commentationem de Studio Matheseos Recte Instituendo" to illustrate the close similarities in several conceptual and methodological respects.

In Chapter 7, revolutionary aspects of demonstration are considered. I turn to reflect upon Kant's enterprise by drawing attention to dimensions of the novel hypotheses of Copernicus and Galileo in order to indicate the sort of things that, although Kant perhaps did not know firsthand, his work nevertheless was influenced by. I suggest in 7.A that Copernicus' novel hypothesis is not so much a matter of astronomical content as a transformation in the prevailing so-called Aristotelian disciplinary matrix, the hierarchical organization of the liberal arts; Copernicus' novel hypothesis is an attempt to review and instruct the physical part of astronomy by arguments from the mathematical part of astronomy. Precisely because the traditional hierarchy of liberal arts regarded mathematics as a secondary science, Copernicus' mathematical demonstration was initially supposed to constitute no threat to the traditional physical account of astronomy endorsed by the Church, among others. Copernicus' *De Revolutionibus* was not viewed by his contemporaries as revolutionary (in the modern sense of the word). Interestingly, since Kant believes that mathematics had entered onto the secure path of a science already with the Greeks, he failed to realize Copernicus' novelty in this important respect, a consequence of which is that it casts further into question the historical dimensions and grounding of Kant's argument about how and when mathematics in fact found its way onto the secure path.

Then, in 7.B, I turn to Galileo, whom Kant learned of firsthand, and in summary from Wolff. Galileo is commonly pointed to when illustrious exponents of the hypothetico-deductive method are sought. Whether Kant was motivated by Galileo, in particular, is indeed hard to say, although Kant refers to him in an imperfect rendition of the history of the experimental method. Following recent work on Galileo, one can give added support to the view that as Kant envisages his contribution—not contrary to an Aristotelian and a priori program—a new kind of demonstration was required to connect the a priori and empirical dimensions of experience. Galileo's novel hypothesis, seen in this light, consists in the introduction of a new method of demonstration, without which the empirical dimension of one's claims could not be proven. The new demonstrative argument is called the demonstrative regress, and later in this study I show that the structure of a transcendental argument—Kant's novel hypothesis of demonstration—shares a similar strategy with that demonstrative regress of Galileo, and elegantly formulated by Newton in the *Opticks*.

In Chapter 8, having pressed the idea of novel hypotheses with regard, first and foremost, to Copernicus, and then to Galileo, I turn to examine Kant's analogous project, on the outlines set forth. The project then becomes twofold; first, I examine the details of the novel hypothesis in terms of the *synthetic a priori* judgments that characterize the foundation of every enterprise Kant believed worthy of calling a science—metaphysics among them—and to indicate how that strategy follows the novel hypothesis of method, outlined in Newton's *Opticks*. By insisting that the foundation of a science consists in synthetic a priori judgments, and following the Copernican analogy, and the inversion of traditional metaphysics, Kant finds himself saddled with a conceptually new problem. How does one prove the validity of judgments that claim to be infallibly certain while, because of their fundamentally synthetic character, cannot be reduced to judgments of logic? Kant's novel hypothesis leads him to ground a system of thought—not along familiar reductionistic programs like that of Leibniz and Wolff, but rather—in judgments whose ultimate justification is not the principle of contradiction. He arrived at this position by extending the traditionally accepted range of synthetical propositions on the one hand, and by driving a wedge between a priori and analytic judgments on the other. The result was the isolation of a new class of judgments that although necessary were not analytic, although necessary were not reducible to judgments of logic. This represents Kant's novel hypothesis of a peculiarly conditional kind of necessity. The suggestion itself was not as new as Kant would wish us to think, but the transformation in point of view—the *Umänderung der Denkart*—forces us to reinterpret this distinction in a new light.

Finally, in Chapter 9, I turn to the predicament of *demonstration* with which Kant now found himself. If the ultimate justification, or demonstration, of the foundation of a science did not rest on a logical principle, the principle of contradiction, then what defense could be given for maintaining the position set forth? Kant's novel hypothesis succeeded in reappraising the very idea of what a demonstration is, and perhaps, if anything, represents the strongest defense of Kant's claim to a revolutionary contribution on the analogy—not with Coperncius—but with Newton.

In 9.A I argue that, in the theory of demonstration propounded by Aristotle in the *Posterior Analytics*, the principles of a system are undemonstrable precisely because they are immediate, self-evident, or obvious. For Kant, however, the principles of his system are not merely capable of but in need of a demonstration. The fundamental judgments of a science, are immediate in some sense, but not obvious. And the demonstration of a principle, the exhibition of the validity of a principle, consists in showing the application of that principle to possible experience. The need to demonstrate principles makes clear Kant's predicament in formulating his novel hypothesis. For since Reason has insight only into that which it has put into nature, then Reason must be unaware, and so instructed, both of the nature of its predicament in general, and the situation in particular. If human theoretical knowledge rests upon this *Umänderung der Denkart*, then evidently we are knowing without knowing that we know, that Reason requires a demonstration to reveal that and what it brings to experience, on the analogy with Copernicus' hypothesis—by examining how it is that objects must conform to our cognitive apparatus—and on the analogy with Newton's demonstration, the validity of the principles are necssary but only in a relational sense, since they express the conditions that must be supposed to account for the contents of the given experience.

In 9.B, I examine the "Metaphysical Deduction" of the *Critique* and show how Kant sought to imitate Newton's method of analysis, or the empiricist's inductive method, to arrive at the categories—the (unschematized) principles. In 9.C, I detail the "Transcendental Deduction" and show how Kant sought to imitate Newton's method of synthesis, or the rationalist deductive procedures, to justify his insight into the principles. The details of hypothesis and deduction express the revolution—on the order to Newton's achievement—that he believed he effected in metaphysics on analogy with the one he perceived to have been effected in natural science.

CHAPTER 2

Kant's Use of the Term "Revolution"

IN KANT'S WRITINGS OF 1793, 1795, AND 1797, HE USES THE TERM "REVOLUTION" to describe what he regards to be a violent and absolutely impermissible sociopolitical practice since it undermines the very possibility of sovereignty. On the other hand, the proliferation of anecdotes suggests unmistakably that Kant sympathized with both the American and French revolutions, and in the B Preface of 1787, Kant countenances the term "revolution" as a positive and enthusiastic way to express his own assessment of his momentous critique of theoretical knowledge. Can these two apparently conflicting positions be reconciled? In order to clarify what Kant believed about his own contribution to philosophy, an examination of the uses he makes of the term "revolution" will prove useful.

2.A. Why Kant Envisioned His *Critique of Pure Reason* to be a Revolution

"With respect to his use of the term 'revolution', Kant is strictly a modern and not a traditionalist; by 'revolution' he does not mean a cyclical change or an ebb and flow, or a return to some better antecedent state, but rather a radical forward step that makes a clean and thorough break with the past."[1] So writes I. Bernard Cohen in his recent work *Revolutions in Science*. The sense that Cohen detects seems appropriate to account for Kant's use of revolution and even *Veränderung* in the *Critique of Pure Reason*; but other uses of this parlance, both in earlier writings, and later, complicates and enriches our view of what revolution meant to Kant, and leads us to envisage, for him, the political and social context of epistemology and metaphysics. For it is indeed worth asking why Kant chooses to illuminate his innovative contribution to metaphysics by employing the political metaphor of revolution.

In order to understand Kant's views on revolution, scholars have tended to focus upon writings in 1793 and following, where Kant's use of revolution is most frequent. The genre of writings in which the word appears is broadly political, reflecting the ongoing controversies about the French Revolution of 1789 et sequentia. The familiar debate about Kant's understanding of revolution is to resolve the apparent paradox that, on the one hand, Kant was a well-known sympathizer of the political revolutions of his time that sought to establish constitutional government and thereby gave expression to what he believed was the progress of history, to individual emancipation—freedom—in the enlightened community, while on the other hand, his writings seem to state unmistakably that he stood opposed to the practice of revolution since it undermined the very structure and integrity of sovereignty itself. Thus, the issue has been to make sense of Kant$_1$, the sympathizer of revolutions, with Kant$_2$, the writer who declares revolutionary acts absolutely impermissible. Can these two dispositions be reconciled without pain of inconsistency?

Recently, Lewis White Beck has argued that the positions can be largely reconciled, but some inconsistency remains. He accepts Kant's "moral enthusiasm for the French Revolution which his formalistic moral system does not justify."[2] Beck grants that Kant's teleological conception of history envisages the final purpose of the world to be moral, not eudaimonistic; thus, the political revolutions that affirmed individual moral worth were seen as an indispensable step in the progress of history to an enlightened community, and thus the fulfillment of moral purpose. But, the tension which persists, Beck believes, is a consequence of the inadequacy of Kantian ethics to deal with the painful problems of conflicting duties.[3] Sidney Axinn shares much of Beck's position but supposes that the apparent inconsistency disappears. To those who believe that Kant cannot hold both of these attitudes, he argues by analogy; "After the painful death of a dear friend it is quite possible, in fact it is a commonplace, to regret the death and yet be glad that the friend did not remain alive to suffer extended final agonies. Kant had both of these attitudes toward all legal governments, including that of Louis XVI."[4] Thus, Axinn's resolution is to suppose that although Kant indeed regretted the violent revolutions, he envisaged them as indispensable to moral progress, and thus sympathized with their program. Atwell, argued, contra Beck, but closer to Axinn, that the two dispositions are consistent; contra Axinn, however, Atwell found the motivation for Kant's embrace of revolution was neither directed toward the specific actions nor consequences, but the universal and disinterested sympathy of those people who had nothing to gain by the revolution, since the sympathy is a sure sign of a moral disposition in man, and thus a sign of the moral progress of human history. The reason why Kant takes this sympathy to be indicative of our moral disposition is that ". . . the publicized principles of the Revolution were nearly the same as the genuinely valid principles of morals and politics. . . ."[5] C. Dyke responded to Beck and Axinn, suggesting that the inconsistency might be overcome from another point of view. Granting the Kantian ideal of a Kingdom of Ends, whose attainment Kant himself denies, our aims in the here-and-now search to achieve the second best result. Revolution for Kant, as Dyke seems to put it, was not unacceptable as a practice, granting an imperfect world and an inherently unattainable Kingdom of Ends to which we are all, nevertheless, morally drawn.[6]

How can these positions help us gain a deeper and clearer understanding of what revolution meant to Kant when he proudly declares his *Critique of Pure Reason* as effecting one, two years prior to the French Revolution? Kant seems to think two different things when he uses the expression "revolution": (1) [earlier–pre-1789] a course of action, the result of which affirmed human moral dignity, freedom, in the instituting of a constitution, which at once signaled, in the sympathy of disinterested people, the affirmation of our moral disposition and thereby the progress of history; (2) [later–post-1789] a violent act of rebellion that undermines the integrity of sovereignty itself. When Kant writes the B Preface to the *Critique of Pure Reason* in 1787, and illuminates his work by regarding it to effect a revolution in the procedure or method that prevailed in metaphysics, he is thinking of revolution in the first sense. And even if we grant to Kant the possible permissibility of violent rebellions in exceptional cases—since at least in one passage in the essay on "Theory and Practice" Kant comes very close to accepting the permissibility of a people's rebellion in the most grave and extraordinary circumstances such as state enforcement of religion, compulsion to unnatural sins, or assassination, and only after he denies the right to rebellion in general—it is hard to believe that his celebration of the *Critique of Pure Reason* as effecting a revolution in metaphysics embraces this ambiguous sense defined by revolution in the second sense.

The hypothesis advanced here is that Kant is thinking about the American Revolution of 1776, and to a lesser extent the Glorious Revolution of 1688 whose centennial was upon him, when he approvingly refers to his historical achievement in terms of a political model of revolution. Despite his conservative demeanor, Kant recognizes an emancipation of the individual, through the declaration of an independence and freedom, in an attempt to realize the rights of man. He could not simply sanction revolution as a legitimate principle of action; and he neither encouraged nor sanctioned revolution in Prussia, nor did he openly advocate such practices. But clearly Kant sympathized with the aims of the revolutionaries so far as they sought to secure individual freedom, and thus fulfill our ultimate political purpose—of perpetual peace—by creating social organizations in which reason legislates over all by legislating from within.

Kant's reputation for support of the American Revolution is well known. The anecdote, even if false, of Kant's meeting Green, as told by the biographer and friend Jachmann, testifies firsthand to Kant's enthusiasm for it. According to that anecdote, Kant was giving a defense of the principles of the American Revolution when an Englishman, named Green, took offense and challenged Kant to a duel! Kant, without taking Green's challenge seriously, clearly enunciated the good reasons for holding support of his view. Green was evidently so taken by the clarity of the arguments that, instead, he invited Kant over to his home, and so began their close friendship.[7]

Kant's support of the French Revolution is even more well-known than his support for the revolution in America. Heine,[8] and later Marx and Engels, singled out Kant as *the* philosopher of the French Revolution.[9] Rumors repeatedly affirmed Kant's support of the French Revolution. In the well-known letter from Biester to Kant in 1793, the minister announces relief—and thereby testifies to the extent of the rumors—upon reading Kant's essay on "Theory and Practice." He expresses relief because he had supposed that Kant supported the French Revolution and believes those rumors are refuted in Kant's essay. In that publication, and in others, the case indeed can be made that Kant repeatedly rejected the practice of revolution as permissible conduct. In Kant's writings of 1793, 1795, and 1797, the overwhelming sentiment is to regard revolution in a negative, if not perjorative light. Revolution is equated with violence, and is regarded as an illegitimate or impermissible social practice: revolution in the second sense. Minimally, this suggests that even if talk of revolution in France was in the air prior to 1789, it could not adequately account for Kant's enthusiastic disposition toward revolution when he wrote the B Preface in 1787.

The French Revolution of 1789 and following could not have accounted for the positions expressed in the essays of 1784, when the expression "revolution" first appears in his writing, nor could it account for Kant's strategy, illuminating his intellectual contribution to metaphysics, employing the metaphor of revolution, in 1787. Thus, it seems likely that sympathies with the aims of the American Revolution of 1776 lie behind Kant's thought of revolution before 1789, no doubt articulated indirectly in the writings of Rousseau.

In his writings post-1789, following the French Revolution, Kant employs the term "revolution" ambiguously. In some places, he identifies it with the human struggle for freedom and autonomy, realized cosmopolitanly, in fulfilling the highest political ideal of perpetual peace. But most of the time, he is wary and cautious in mentioning it. The word "revolution" is frequently characterized by "violent," and several times Kant explicitly insists upon the sacredness and inviolability of civil constitutions, and thereby declares revolutions—now equated with unjustifiable, violent rebellions, or revolution in the second sense—as absolutely impermissible. How shall we account for this change in sympathy?

Although Kant sympathized with both the American and French revolutions, it seems likely that he had a change of heart, as a result of the Reign of Terror, and the general excesses in France with which he would be far more familiar and well-informed than with the American Revolution. In that letter from J. E. Biester, secretary to Minister von Zedlitz (to whom the *Critique of Pure Reason* is dedicated), and publisher of the *Berlinische Monatsschrift*, rumor of Kant's support for the French Revolution is supposed to be refuted. Biester had published, in September 1793 Kant's essay "On the Common Saying: 'That May Be True in Theory but Not in Practice.' " In his letter dated 5 October 1793, he points to the passage in the second section as confirmation of Kant's refusal to support the French Revolution.[10] In the following passage from that essay, Kant seems to state unmistakably that violent overthrow of a government is absolutely impermissible—a quintessential use of revolution in the second sense:

> It thus follows that all resistance against the supreme legislative power, all incitement of the subjects to violent expressions of discontent, all defiance which breaks out into rebellion, is the greatest and most punishable crime in a commonwealth, for it destroys its very foundations. This prohibition is absolute.[11]

Thus it seems clear that, while Kant held that human struggles for freedom and autonomy, in the social community, counted no less central than the individuals struggle for their own autonomy, in the practical sphere, he rejected the principle of revolution, exposing it for the unmitigated violence and terror that it proves to be. Not only was Kant repulsed by that violence but it seems to have forced him to see that such political rebellion undermines the possibility of a stable polity, indispensable to individual moral development itself. In a word, Kant understands that the consequences of approving of violent revolution are self-stultifying. One cannot right the wrongs and excesses of governance by undermining the institution itself.

It is at this moment that we document Kant's change of heart. The connotations of the word have changed by this tumultuous time, sometime after 1789. The word comes to attain a boldly negative sense the very mention of which sent fear and terror into the hearts of the common people who would endure such mayhem, or what I have called revolution in the second sense. To be sure, some ambiguity remains, and especially in 1798, in the *Contest of the Faculties*, Kant reminds us that he has not forgotten the positive dimension of revolution—in the first sense. But, if Kant held this ambiguous view of revolution in 1787, it is difficult to believe that he would have described his great contribution in terms of it.

Was this Kant who adamantly declares revolutions to be absolutely prohibited the same one who earlier described his achievement of placing metaphysics on the secure path of a science in terms of a revolution which he effected, alongside of the successful revolution in physics—the scientific revolution? Was this the Kant who boasts that he is the revolutionary leader himself, and congratulates himself for having successfully led a revolution so decisive in its impact that it made further revolutions both unnecessary and impossible? When he wrote the essays of 1784, the awful truth of the political revolution had not quite sunk in, perhaps because the atrocities and excesses of the American Revolution remained largely unknown, due to the great distance and intermittent communication of events. This is likely the case, even in the 1787 publication of the B Preface. Otherwise, we would wonder how Kant could choose to describe his contribution to the history of intellectual thought on the model of what he himself came to regard as a monstrous and absolutely impermissible atrocity. So far as the evidence seems telling, Kant changed his mind about the nature of revolution. Subsequent to the writing of the B Preface, Kant never seems to have referred to his critique of pure reason in terms of a revolution.

2.B. Occurrences of Revolution Prior to the B Preface of the *Critique* (Pre-1789)

According to the index to the Academy edition, the *Allgemeiner Kantindex*, compiled under the supervision of Gottfried Martin,[12] which informs the reader of the number of times certain expressions are used but regretfully lists no pagination [i.e., "revolution" is used three times in volumes 1 and 2!], the expression "revolution" appears six times in volume 3, all of which can be found in the B Preface to the first *Critique*, and thus were published in the year 1787. In order more fully to make my case that Kant's use of "revolution" is equivocal, but only after 1789, I examine the pre-1789 writings, which provide evidence for the broadly positive and supportive attitude which the word conjured for Kant. The ambiguity arises in writings post-1789 when the word produced very powerful and terrifying feelings in Kant's community, and Kant was forced to accept a negative, dangerous, and alarming connotation that the word aroused, right alongside of another and positive sense, which had long before become entrenched in his vocabulary. Kant's earlier view is generally approbative—revolution in the first sense. But, sometime after 1789, Kant came to overlap that meaning of revolution with a second sense without ever abandoning the earlier view. Only in the writings post-1789 is Kant's attitude toward revolution made difficult because he uses the word equivocally. This equivocity is nowhere evidenced in the pre-1789 writings; in those earlier uses Kant affirms his laudatory support for revolution in the first sense.

The difficulty of understanding the compatibility of revolution$_1$ and revolution$_2$ emerges as a result of the tension between a sympathy for signs of moral realization (equals first sense), a commitment to which he never abandons, and yet the refusal to support the violence that undermines the institution of sovereignty, thereby making rightful rule difficult to reestablish (equals second sense), which became the troublesome but more familiar meaning of the term in the early 1790s. Biester's worry, and relief, suggests clearly that revolution was a word that now provoked very negative and constrained feelings in the upper-hierarchical command that approved and published Kant's writings. This leads me to suppose that if the *Critique of Pure Reason* was to undergo a second edition, not in 1787, but sometime after 1789, say 1793, it seems unbelievable, granting this hypothesis, that Kant would have re-Prefaced his metaphysics in terms of a revolution even if he indeed would continue to believe that his work had effected one. To make this case more fully, I turn first to the three earliest occurrences of revolution, which appear in essays published in 1784; two references to revolution in "Idea for a Universal History with a Cosmopolitan Purpose" and one reference in the essay "What is Enlightenment?" After examining these three references, I proceed to examine all of its occurrences in the first *Critique*, and finally survey about two dozen later references, in writings published in 1793, 1795, 1797, and 1798.

In the first of two references to revolution, published in the *Berlinische Monatsschrift* in 1784 under the title *Idee zu einer allgemeinen Geschichte in weltburgerlicher Absicht*, the word, used in the plural, suggests stages of development to some optimal circumstance, characterized by self-sufficiency.[13] Thus, revolution is used to represent stages in progression to a morally superior world. The revolutions are not really the plan of men so much as they are the intentions of nature whose ultimate end is projected as moral realization for the whole community, and thus its "cosmopolitan purpose"—or what I am calling revolution in the first sense. I think here we can see that Kant does not object to revolutionary activity because he envisages these human struggles to be understood in a wider context in which they are seen to be instruments of nature's intention. This suggests to me that he could not hold blameworthy those humans whose efforts were at nature's behest, and intended to fulfill some greater purpose of her own design.

> All wars are accordingly so many attempts (not indeed by the intention of men, but by the intention of nature) to bring about new relations between states, and, by the destruction or at least the dismemberment of old entities, to create new ones. But these new bodies, either in themselves or alongside one another, will in turn be able to survive, and will thus necessarily undergo further revolutions of a similar sort, till finally, partly by an optimal internal arrangement of the civil constitution, and partly by common external agreement and legislation, a state of affairs is created which, like a civil commonwealth, can maintain itself automatically.[14]

In the second occurrence of revolution in this essay, the expression, again, represents a series of radical stages that lead to the highest development of the individual within the most enlightened social/political community—a universal cosmopolitan existence. Thus, revolution, through a political connotation, comes to characterize stages of human moral development, in the context of social developments of communities, constituted by human moral agents. This, again, is revolution in the first sense:

> Although this political body exists for the present only in the roughest of outlines, it nonetheless seems as if a feeling is beginning to stir in all its members, each of which has an interest in maintaining the whole. And this encourages the hope that, after many revolutions, with all their transforming effects, the highest purpose of nature, a universal cosmopolitan existence, will at last be realized as the matrix within which all the original capacities of the human race may develop.[15]

In the third, and last, reference to revolution prior to the B Preface in the first *Critique*—this time in the essay published in the *Berlinische*

Monatsschrift one month later than the essay on universal history, entitled *"Beantwortung der Frage: Was ist Aufklärung?"* or "What is Enlightenment?"—Kant calls upon the word to clarify the positive contribution to defects in political sovereignty while at once announcing its deficiencies.[16] The revolution can put an end to iniquitous political regimes, but it cannot effect the positive character of enlightenment, which is freedom—still, revolution in the first sense, because although such activity will not guarantee enlightenment, it's sense is still not affected by the negative prohibitions:

> Thus, a public can only achieve enlightenment slowly. A revolution may well put an end to autocratic despotism and to rapacious or power-seeking oppression, but it will never produce a true reform in ways of thinking. Instead, new prejudices, like the ones they replaced, will serve as a leash to control the great unthinking mass. For enlightenment of this kind, all that is needed is freedom. And the freedom in question is the most innocuous form of all—freedom to make public use of one's reason in all matters.[17]

In this passage, Kant reveals his disdain for both "autocratic despotism" and a "rapacious or power-seeking oppression"; his systematic commitments have already convinced him that fundamental ingredients in human moral development are either enhanced or obstructed by the political situation in which one finds oneself. But, moral realization, the fulfillment of moral agency, rests not ultimately with the political domain. Since there is no guarantee that obedience to duty, to Reason in its practical sphere, will arise for everyone within some political circumstance or other. In short, the political structure, although useful and perhaps necessary for full moral development, is not sufficient for it. This passage suggests that insofar as it is useful or necessary, revolution is to be commended and applauded, but insofar as it is supposed to be sufficient as a guarantee that those affected by it will discover the reason that guides it, for this revolution can provide no sufficient condition. Revolution is, thus, no panacea but it is a sign of a progressive and advancing moral realization infecting the whole community.

2.C. Occurrences of Revolution in the B Preface of the *Critique* (1787)

The publication of the B Preface to the *Critique of Pure Reason* in 1787 places a shift of emphasis on the employment of revolution, unlike the earlier uses, in two ways. First, rather than suggesting radical stages in development leading to some definitive and optimal end, the word is now used to characterize the definitive end itself. Second, revolution is now applied to matters epistemological and metaphysical, and the ethical dimension of stages leading to communal autonomy is nowhere evidenced. The omission of the overt ethical implications of the parlance so strikingly present in the essays of 1784 is not surprising when we remember the focus of the *Critique* on theoretical knowledge (i.e., as opposed to the practical), for the practical domain is expressly relegated to a separate study. It is worth underscoring, however, that at the time of this writing—roughly 1787—Kant envisages a strongly positive meaning expressed by the term "revolution," for otherwise, it is difficult to see why he would characterize his own great contribution to philosophy in these terms, most especially after rethinking that work (published first in 1781) for more than half a decade.

The word "revolution"—appearing six times in the B Preface—cannot here represent a series of stages because, applied to the development of mathematics and physics, Kant seeks to isolate that definitive and radical transformation that set these enterprises on *der sichere Gang einer Wissenschaft*, on "the sure path of a science." Once that royal road has been secured, there is no further nor possible need for a revolution. The expression "revolution" appears nowhere in the preface to the A edition, nor elsewhere in the *Critique*. Here, in this text, the approbative force, the powerful optimism expressed in that parlance—revolution in the (first) sense—is advanced.

In the B Preface, Kant proceeds to investigate the condition that enabled mathematics and physics—in which reason yields theoretical knowledge—to become sciences. Kant begins by supposing that these enterprises guaranteed certainty in their endeavors and thus merited description as sciences. He explains this condition as a revolution. The sciences have achieved, in his estimation, a remarkable progress. Thus, revolution becomes somewhat a term of endearment, in accounting for what is essential: the advancement of reason in history, stages by which human beings came to discover the ultimate structure of things, in their moral nature. For Kant, this was no less nature's intention than was nature's intention to call us to fulfill the *summum bonum*—for the highest good (*bonum supremum*) was no less the complete good (*bonum consummatum*). The complete good includes not only the demand for happiness in proportion in virtue, but also the realization of this ideal, within each person's reason, as the good society, where a republican constitution rightly prevails, and thus guides us. The *Critique of Pure Reason* is in no way inconsistent with the design and fulfillment of moral purpose. In this passage, Kant first takes up mathematics, contrasts it with logic—whereby reason has merely itself to deal with—and insists that it had to "construct for itself that royal road." At Bxi:

> . . . I believe that it [sc. mathematics] remained, especially among the Egyptians, in the groping stage, and that the transformation must have been due to a revolution brought about by the happy thought of a single man, the experiment which he devised marking out the path upon which the science must enter, and by following which, secure progress throughout all time and in endless expansion is infallibly secured.

Kant immediately turns to clarify the status of this revolution by contrasting it with the navigational discovery of the passage around the Cape of Good Hope. The revolution in mathematics was an intellectual one. Continuing at Bxi:

> The history of this intellectual revolution—far more important than the discovery of the passage round the celebrated Cape of Good Hope—and of its fortunate author, has not been preserved.

The revolution in mathematics consisted in the brilliant discovery of the man who demonstrated the properties of an isosceles triangle, be it Thales or someone else. For Kant, geometry marks the revolution in mathematics. It is not a discovery of the figure, nor an analysis of the bare concept, that marks the ascension to the highway or royal road of science. The revolution consists in bringing out what was necessarily implied in the concepts that he had formed a priori and had put into the figure in the construction by which he presented it to himself. Again, following at Bxi:

> . . . Diogenes Laertius, in handing down an account of these matters [sc. concerning the development of geometry] . . . does at least show that the memory of the revolution [Veränderung], brought about by the glimpse of this new path, must have seemed to mathematicians of such outstanding importance as to cause it to survive the tide of oblivion.

Now Kant turns to consider the condition by which "natural science" or "physics" found its way to the secure path of a science, and a revolution of a comparable sort is noted. At Bxii:

> In this case [sc. natural science/physics] also, the discovery can be explained as being the sudden outcome of an intellectual revolution.

Then, Kant proceeds with an imperfect rendition of the history of the empirical method, and concludes at Bxiii–Bxiv:

> Even physics, therefore, owes the beneficent revolution in its point of view entirely to the happy thought, that while reason must seek in nature, not fictitiously ascribe to it, whatever as not being knowable through reason's own resources has to be learnt, if learnt at all, only from nature, it must adopt as its guide, in so seeking, that which it has itself put into nature. It is thus that the study of nature has entered on the secure path of a science, after having for so many centuries been nothing but a process of merely random groping.

In his last uses of the noun "revolution" in this text, Kant restates his claim, and from this perspective, recasts his philosophical enterprise within the context of his discovery of the revolution that placed mathematics and physics on the path to certainty. The term "revolution" Kant employs, not to describe a series of stages, as did his use of revolution in the essay on the "Idea for a Universal History with a Cosmopolitan Purpose." Here, revolution is supposed to connote both a "single" and "sudden" transformation. Kant then describes his project following his articulation of the discovery that made the revolutionary achievement in mathematics and physics possible. At Bxvi:

> The examples of mathematics and natural science, which by a single and sudden revolution have become what they now are, seem to me sufficiently remarkable to suggest our considering what may have been the essential features in the changed point of view by which they have so greatly benefited. Their success should incline us, at least by way of experiment, to imitate their procedure, so far as the analogy which, as species of rational knowledge, they bear to metaphysics may permit.

The same strategy is then repeated, underscoring the meaning of revolution as radical upheaval, at Bxxii. In this quintessential use, Kant not only insists that his purpose is to effect a revolution but at once reveals himself to be its leader. The *Critique*, then, becomes his stated revolutionary plans:

> This attempt to alter the procedure which has hitherto prevailed in metaphysics, by completely revolutionizing it in accordance with the examples set by the geometers and physicists, forms indeed the main purpose of this critique of pure speculative reason.

In each of the occurences of revolution in the first *Critique*, the first sense is adhered to; the achievement of effecting a revolution is laudable and worthy of our greatest esteem.

2.D. Occurrences of Revolution Subsequent to the B Preface of the *Critique* (Post-1787)

When Kant describes his constructive contribution to theoretical knowledge, he describes it in terms of a revolution he believes he is effecting. The result, like other revolutions in knowledge, placed human theoretical enterprises on the secure path of a science. The connotation of the parlance is clearly approbative. But, after the French Revolution of 1789, and following, reports of such extreme and atrocious behavior produced much ambivalence in Kant's mind, and in those of other contemporaries, about the benefit and desirability of revolution. Overall, revolution seems to suggest radical upheaval, as it does in the first *Critique*. But, since Kant finds himself unable to embrace revolution as either a useful political strategy, or as morally acceptable, the word cannot have retained the positive sense that seems to be suggested by his choice in 1787, when reappraising his *Critique of Pure Reason*.

Nevertheless, he still continues to see the advent of revolution as an attempt to realize the dignity of human moral worth founded upon both an ultimate moral equality and freedom. He notes the sympathy with which the revolutions have been greeted by those not involved in the particular disputes. He suggests that we may account for this popular sympathy by realizing a deep moral sentiment within man. In the essay of 1798, the *Contest of Faculties*, he attempts to embrace the idea of revolution but only in terms of an evolution of a constitution governed by natural right. The following occurrences suggest both Kant's change of disposition with regard to the feelings that revolution evoked for him, and yet also a continued ambivalence to the idea.

Of the forty-three occurrences of the word "revolution" in the Kantian corpus, according to the *Allgemeiner Kantindex*, nine of those occurrences can be found in volumes 1–3. Sixteen references can be found in volume 6, fifteen in volumes 7 and 8, and three are contained in volume 9.[18] I cannot here offer an exhaustive presentation, nor would it suit the purposes of this study, which focuses upon the first *Critique*. I turn now, however, to survey about two dozen of these latter thirty-four references in volumes 6–9 to demonstrate the increasing ambiguity that

Kant felt about revolution. I begin with occurrences in the 1793 publication of *Religion Within the Limits of Reason Alone*, next consider the 1795 *Perpetual Peace*, then the *Metaphysics of Morals* of 1797, and finally the occurrences of "revolution" are examined in the 1798 publication, *Contest of Faculties*.

There are at least seven uses of "revolution" in *Religion innerhalb der Grenzen der blossen Vernunft* or *Religion Within the Limits of Reason Alone*, published in 1793.[19] The following occurrences all appear in book 3, "The Victory of the Good over the Evil Principle, and the Founding of a Kingdom of God on Earth." Within that book, references are found in those sections which discuss transitions from an ecclesiastical faith to the exclusive sovereignty of "pure religious faith," and "historical transitions" to the establishment of the good principle on earth. In the relevant section, he is thinking about how the presently deficient condition in states will unite and overcome those limitations in order to achieve that kingdom of God. He understands that some sort of revolution is required, but cannot advocate such a procedure because of its dangers, most especially to the very undermining of "freedom."

The breakdown of the ecclesiastical faith is announced by the disappearance of what Kant calls "the humiliating distinction between laity and clergy." Such a distinction obfuscates the enlightened vision of individual moral worth, and thus an underlying human equality. That "equality arises through true freedom." The ecclesiastical structure suggests a hierarchy of moral worth, and undermines moral affirmation expressed in autonomy alone which grants no special privilege to clerical status. When the ecclesiastical hierarchy disappears, Kant insists, the result will not be anarchy, but rather "each obeys the (non-statutory) law which he prescribes to himself [and] he must regard this law as the will of a World-Ruler revealed to him through Reason, a will which by invisible means unites all under one government into a state—a state previously and inadequately represented and prepared for by the visible church."[20] But, the promised land of "Religion within the Limits of Reason Alone," to which historical process is advancing, will not be achieved or furthered by violent revolution. As Kant says, using revolution in the second sense:

> All this is not to be expected from an external revolution, because such an upheaval produces its effects tempestuously and violently, an effect, quite dependent on circumstances. Moreover, whatever mistake has once been made in the establishment of a new constitution, is regretfully retained throughout hundreds of years, since it can no longer by changed or at least only through a new (and at any time dangerous) revolution. . . . [But, the pure religion of reason is continually occurring divine revelation, and is advan-

cing through gradual reforms. . . . As for revolutions which might hasten this progress, they rest in the hands of Providence and cannot be ushered in according to plan without damage to freedom.[21]

In this same work, Kant proceeds to extend revolution to describe transitions in prevailing religious mentalities. In his attempt to provide a general church history, Kant describes Christianity as effecting a thoroughgoing revolution in doctrines of faith.

We cannot, therefore, do otherwise than begin general church history, if it is to constitute a system, with the origins of Christianity, which, completely forsaking the Judaism from which it sprang, and grounded upon a wholly new principle, effected a thoroughgoing revolution in doctrines of faith.[22]

This willingness to apply revolution to transitions in religious doctrine is in accord with Kant's modern rather than traditionalist approach—to use Cohen's distinction—to envisage revolution as meaning radical upheaval. And, at once, it seems to resound revolution in what I have been calling the the first or earlier sense. The application of the term to upheavals in religious doctrine is reaffirmed in the following passage in which the term appears no less than three more times:

Now at the time of the revolution in question there were present among the people [the Romans], who ruled the Jews and had spread into their very domain, a learned public from whom the history of the political events of that period has indeed been handed down to us through an unbroken series of writers. . . . Yet they made no mention, as contemporaries, either of these miracles or of the revolution which the miracles produced (in respect to religion) in the people under their dominion, though the revolution had taken place quite as publicly.[23]

In the 1793 essay published in the *Berlinische Monatsschrift*, under the editorship of J. E. Biester, "On the Common Saying: 'This May be true in Theory, but it does not Apply in Practice,' " the word "revolution" appears at least twice. Both occurrences appear in the same section that Biester, in his letter of 5 October 1793, believed confirmed his view that Kant could not be counted among the supporters of the French Revolution. Kant announces an absolute prohibition on violent revolution since it destroys the very foundations of the commonwealth. In that section, Kant insists, against what he calls estimable opponents, like Achenwall, that "the subject is still not entitled to offer counter-resistance" even if the head of state "has violated the original contract by authorizing the government to act tyrannically."[24] Kant's reason seems to be this: ". . . under an existing civil constitution. . . [the people have] no longer any right to judge how the constitution should be administered."[25] Kant hopes to clarify his stand by wondering about our view of the leaders of revolutions, had they failed. His conclusion is that these leaders could not be thought any better than great political criminals:

> And it can scarcely be doubted that if the revolutions whereby Switzerland, the United Netherlands, or even Great Britain, won their much admired constitutions had failed, the leaders of their history would regard the execution of their celebrated founders as no more than the deserved punishment of great political criminals.[26]

Kant then immediately reaffirms his stance that revolutions are absolutely impermissible because they undermine the possibility of a secure and lawful constitution—revolution in the quintessential statement of the second sense:

> But it is clear that these people [i.e., leaders of political revolutions] have done the greatest degree of wrong in seeking their rights in this way, even if we admit that such a revolution did no injustice to a ruler who had violated a specific basic agreement with the people. . . . For such procedures, if made into a maxim, make all awful constitutions insecure and produce a state of complete lawlessness (status naturalis) where all rights cease at least to be effectual.[27]

Could this be the Kant who celebrated his glorious accomplishment in 1781, as the solution to every problem in metaphysics, now and forever, in the A Preface, and again in the new Preface of 1787 by describing his achievement as a revolution? Was not the Kant of 1787 the man who claimed not merely to be a revolutionary but indeed its leader? No doubt, Kant had modified his enthusiasm, at least for the public rhetoric.

In 1795, Kant published an essay under the title *Zum ewigen Frieden. Ein philosophischer Entwurf*, commonly known as *Perpetual Peace*, presumably in response to the signing of the Treaty of Basle on 5 April 1795.[28] In three references to revolution in this work, Kant even more closely equates violence, and thereby unacceptable behavior with it. In the first occurrence, which appears in the second section of that essay, Kant makes clear the goal of constitutional government as the approximation to its "republican potentiality," which unifies the state into a structure of legislator and legislated, and thereby mirrors the internal structure of self-legislating morality. Democracy, on the other hand, is not only more prone to revolution, but as Kant observes, the required "republican" attitude is impossible since everyone under a democracy wishes to be the ruler. Thus, we see Kant using revolution in the second sense.

> For this reason, it is more difficult in an aristocracy than in a monarchy to reach this one and only perfectly lawful kind of constitution, while it is possible in a democracy only by means of violent revolution[29]

In the first appendix to this essay, the same sentiment is expressed, that revolution is violent and impermissible, again in the second sense:

> If, however, a more lawful constitution were attained by unlawful means, i.e. by a violent revolution, resulting from a previous bad constitution, it would then no longer be permissible to lead the people back to the original one, even although everyone who had interfered with the old constitution by violence or conspiracy would rightly have been subject to the penalties of rebellion during the revolution itself.[30]

In 1797, when Kant published *Die Metaphysik der Sitten*, or *Metaphysics of Morals*, he was preoccupied, in part, with determining how legitimate constitutional rule is reinstituted following violent revolution.[31] Since the violent revolution undermines the very institution of legitimate power, as he sees it, there is great difficulty is reestablishing secure lawful authority. In the section entitled "General Remarks on the Legal Consequences of the Nature of the Civil Union," Kant declares in a footnote that the most monstrous act perpetrated through revolution—in the second sense—and rebellion is not the killing of the monarch, but the formal execution of the monarch; this act arouses "moral" dread in one's soul because it represents "the complete reversal of all concepts of right."

> But of all the outrages attending a revolution through rebellion, even the murder of the monarch is not the worst. . . . It is the formal execution of a monarch which must arouse dread in any soul imbued with ideas of human right. . . . [This feeling is] moral, being our reaction to the complete reversal of all concepts of right.[32]

When the constitution falls into disrepair, as will happen from time to time, the only legitimate form of change is that enacted by the sovereign through reform, but never by revolution—in the second sense—which is enacted by the people:

Any alteration to a defective political constitution, which may certainly be necessary at times, can thus be carried out only by the sovereign himself through *reform*, but not through revolution by the people. And if any such alteration takes place, it can only effect the executive power, not the legislature.[33]

In a passage directly following, the word "revolution" appears not less than four times. The issue under discussion concerns reinstituting lawful authority after a successful revolution. The sense of "revolution" is replete with ambivalence.

Furthermore, if a revolution has succeeded and a new constitution has been established, the unlawfulness of its origins and success cannot free the subjects from the obligation to accommodate themselves as good citizens to the new order of things. . . . The dethroned monarch, if he survives such a revolution, cannot be taken to task for his earlier management of the state, far less punished for it. This applies so long as he has retired to the status of a citizen, preferring his own peace to the hazards of abandoning his position and embarking as a pretender on the enterprise of restoration, whether through secretly instigated counter-revolution or the support of other powers. . . . [It must be left to international right to decide whether other powers may join to aid the fallen monarch] in order that the people's crimes not go unpunished or remain as a scandal in the eyes of other states, and whether they are entitled or called upon to overthrow a constitution established in any other state by revolution, and to restore the old one by forcible means.[34]

Beck pointed out that the fervid denial of the right of revolution, in this passage, is "historically focussed not against the Estates General and the successor government, but upon efforts at the counterrevolution and restoration of the Bourbons. Thus Kant specifically denounces the right claimed by other sovereigns to intervene in French affairs so as to undo the Revolution."[35] What Beck has so sensitively grasped is the degree to which the specific events of that revolution played in Kant's reassessment of the very idea of revolution. Attendance to the social context that swayed his attitude toward what was commonly signified by revolution offers a way of understanding Kant's ambivalent attitude in a more revealing way than an analysis of the apparent internal inconsistencies or an appeal to problems in distinguishing between juridical and natural rights.

Later in section fifty-two of the *Metaphysics of Morals*, the permissibility of revolution—in the second sense—is again explicitly rejected:

But revolution under an already existing constitution means the destruction of all relationships governed by civil right, and thus of right altogether.[36]

And this very same sentiment is repeated again in the last and concluding paragraph, under section sixty-two, on cosmopolitan right, supposing revolution in the *second* sense:

But no attempt should be made to put it into practice overnight by revolution i.e. by forcibly overthrowing a defective constitution which has existed in the past; for there would then be an interval of time during which the condition of right would be nullified. If we try instead to give it reality by means of gradual reforms carried out in accordance with definite principles, we shall see that this is the only means of continually approaching the supreme political good—perpetual peace.[37]

In the brief appendix that follows the main text of the *Metaphysics of Morals*, Kant again repeats his views on the sacredness and inviolability of civil constitutions, and simultaneously denies absolutely any right to rebellion or violent revolution—in the second sense.[38]

In 1798, when Kant published *Der Streit der Facultaten* or *Contest of the Faculties*, his ambivalence about revolution evidences itself again.[39] Fully conscious of the miseries and atrocities that result from revolutions, Kant nevertheless wonders from where in human nature does the sympathy for such revolutions emerge. He concludes, in section six, that it could emerge from nothing other than our "moral disposition." This is a late case of revolution in the first sense contrasted with revolution in the second sense, in the same passage:

The revolution which we have seen taking place in our own times in a nation of gifted people may succeed, or it may fail. It may be so filled with misery and atrocities that no right-thinking man would ever decide to make the same experiment again at such a price, even if he could hope to carry it out successfully at the second attempt. But I maintain that this revolution has aroused in the hearts and desires of all spectators who are not themselves caught up in it a *sympathy* which borders almost on enthusiasm, although the very utterance of this sympathy was fraught with danger. It cannot therefore have been caused by anything other than a moral disposition within the human race.[40]

Kant then continues this point by distinguishing between the zeal of the revolutionaries and the disposition of their opponents. His point is that the revolutionaries are motivated by their own concept of right, the implication of which is that their actions are motivated by our moral nature, the affirmation of a freedom resting in moral equality, referring to revolution in an approbative or first sense.

> No pecuniary rewards could inspire the opponents of the revolutionaries with that zeal and greatness of soul which the concept of right alone could produce in them. . . .[41]

In the *Contest of the Faculties*, Kant recognizes the epoch-making influence of Reason in its discovery of the moral domain of human experience, and its expression in the social practices of the state. In this text, Kant envisages the revolutions as consisting in man's attempt to rise up and give expression to the dignity of human freedom, in the political domain. He then makes this point, in section seven, following a distinction between revolution and evolution made by his friend Erhard in an essay entitled "Uber das Recht des Volkes zu einer Revolution."[42] It seems that Kant favors this approach because he wishes to manifest sympathy for the human moral struggle, and is clearly conscious of the negative implications of the term revolution." Thus, I am suggesting here that his resolution to the felt tension of two doctrines—on the one hand, revolution had a deeply significant and positive meaning, while on the other, talk of revolution, following 1789, conjured highly controversial, minimally ambivalent, and maximally outraged feelings—was to transfer the positive or first sense of revolution to the expression "evolution" with whose approbative force it was now endowed.

> The occurrence in question is not, however, a phenomenon of revolution, but (as Erhard puts it) of the evolution of a constitution governed by natural right.[43]

This distinction is mentioned again in the last section of the essay, section ten:

> And this will mean that the state too will reform itself from time to time, pursuing evolution instead of revolution, and will thus make continuing progress.[44]

Thus, when the word "revolution" became too controversial, by 1798, and while still maintaining the ideology of the first sense, which had long become entrenched in his vocabulary and thinking, Kant sought to preserve it by adapting the parlance "evolution" and thereby giving up the usefulness of the word to communicate a positive point. This perspective on revolution Kant did not have in 1787 when he envisioned his

Critique of Pure Reason to be effecting such a revolution. Thus, Kant embraced early on, and continued to embrace throughout, revolution in the first sense, a word that connoted a transition to moral agency, fulfilling cosmopolitan purpose. The more-or-less bloodless Glorious Revolution of 1688 and more distant accounts of the more recent American Revolution of 1776 did not reveal the viciousness inherent in the noble attempt to institute a civil constitution. The fulfillment of human history in enlightened communities, suggested as early as the 1784 essay on "Universal History with a Cosmopolitan Purpose," was never abandoned, in terms of the revolution, but the negative sense—the second sense—which became prevalent as a result of the excesses of the French Revolution, Kant regarded as generally unjustifiable, and could not happily embrace it.

CHAPTER 3

Experiment and the Revolution in Science According to the B Preface of 1787

EVEN IF WE SUPPOSE THAT KANT EXPRESSLY INTENDS TO EFFECT A NEW-tonian revolution in philosophy, and seeks to imitate the model of scientific method embraced by those like Galileo, Torricelli, and Stahl, and articulated in a definitive fashion by Newton, it still remains for us to consider how that method must be refashioned, and thus perhaps distorted, when applied to metaphysics. This becomes all the more apparent when we see Kant characterize the enterprise of science by its integral feature of experiment, whose design he attempts to reproduce for testing metaphysical claims. He uses the term not merely with regard to natural science, but to mathematics as well. To see how *Experimentalmethode* can be accommodated in all these domains, we must come to see how Kant fundamentally transforms the scientific method explicated by Newton.

Experiment either loses its empirical connotations, or remaining identified with the empirical, empirical takes on an unexpectedly abstract sense: Experiment generally seems to mean thought-experiment—since it must be capable of applying to both mathematical constructions in pure intuition, as well as the rate of fall of bodies down an inclined plane. The effect is to weigh almost exclusively on the a priori aspect of the science; and yet we might first suspect that the main denotation of experiment—following even a casual reading of the *Principia*—is a posteriori. Kant's understanding of revolution in science emphasizes the a priori, not the a posteriori. He seeks to reinterpret scientific advance by entirely downplaying the a posteriori dimension, and to bolster his case, misrepresents the expressed intentions of these earlier enterprises. His paranoia is scepticism; the insistence upon certainty drives him to this imbalance.

This maneuver helps to reveal what seems to be a troubling ambiguity in Kant's motivation and strategy, despite his objections to the contrary. Although his rhetoric declares that his experiment is a test, that if his results produced counterexamples, undermining the sought-after confirmation, he would be compelled to dismiss his argument and reformulate another, Kant's a priori rapture blinded him to defects in his own argument. He evidently did not respond well—as the rhetoric insisted—to what ought to have counted as either counterevidence to particular sciences he believed he understood a priori, or the a priori program in general, as a consequence of counterexamples. He did not empirically investigate the sciences or mathematics, any more than he did geography or sailing—other topics on which he wrote. And, however extensive was his reading, he wrote a treatise on physical geography without ever having traveled more than sixty miles or so from his native Königsberg; he wrote on the art of sailing without ever having set sail on the Baltic Sea. And when his claims were challenged by those who lived in parts of the world about which he wrote, or his arguments were opposed by those who empirically practiced the arts of which he wrote, Kant gained a reputation for being a stodgy, narrow-minded thinker who was not easy to reason with—as the critical rhetoric demanded. Although he declares that he admired the success of the sciences and then attempted to construct for metaphysics the science modeled on the students of nature, it rather seems that he came to a conclusion about the a priori structure of experience—because of his eagerness to ensure certainty and thus overcome the sceptical challenge he feared most—and then architectonically superimposed it upon experience. He first became committed to this a priori vision, and as the theory required, placed it as a pattern over the contents of experience to produce a story that he—qua Kant, not qua human creature with a sensible intuition—had already read into experience. In short, he carried out extrinsically what the theory declared requisite intrinsically.

The consequence was that Kant offered to explain motivations and intentions that scientific thinkers never stated; he sought to account for their achievements in terms that he supposed they never rightly understood. That Kant comes to this view for a very understandable reason becomes clear if we entertain one simple supposition: he was wrong. His error consisted principally in his insistence upon imposing the God's eye point of view, which he supposed he discovered, on achievements whose historical contexts escaped him, and defied the very description which he fixed onto them. But, the complexities of historical circumstances could not really trouble him since the a priori program revealed what human activities sought regardless of even the strongest counterevidence, namely, explicit statements of intention to the contrary. He was, I believe, mistaken about their scientific achievements as a direct consequence of his error in supposing that he discovered the God's eye point of view about the structure of a priori subjectivity. This error was on just the same order as that which he made in physical geography, following another a priori insight: when, in 1798, Kant was informed that Napoleon had landed in Egypt, having already determined beforehand—for geopolitical reasons—that he must land in Portugal, Kant indignantly assailed the news report as a "journalistic hoax."[1]

Kant's a priori program, for all of its insight, suffered from an acute myopia. He seems, in general, to have refused to revise his positions even when evidence to the contrary was presented to him. This behavior evokes a suspicion about the empirical or experimental dimension of his metaphysics, and the requisite a posteriori dimension of the scientific revolution that his rhetoric insists that he employ as a model for philosophical thinking. Thus we come to review the critical program, the one that follows the privileged (a priori) point of view: Kant not only believed he understood achievements of others better than they understood their own, but supposed he knew their intentions even when there was no good evidence for it, or indeed, even when such motivations were expressly denied by them.

Take the case for Greek mathematics. Could the case be made for Euclid and his classical contemporaries, and even the earlier archaic predecessors like Thales, that not only did mathematics find its way to the secure road of a science in their times but more importantly achieved that status by their recognition of a structure which they discovered that they themselves imposed upon experience? I believe the answer is clearly no. Although the story is a complex one, it seems fair to say that there is little or no evidence to suggest that the experiment of the earliest geometer(s) consisted in marking out the path of the science by employing a method "to bring out what was necessarily implied in the concepts that he had himself formed *a priori*, and had put into the figure in the construction by which he presented it to himself" (Bxii). The origin of Greek science is more properly identified with the vision that the *kosmos*—a word that comes to mean the ordered whole—has a precise order, and human beings have a *nous* or a consciousness capable of grasping and expressing that order.[2] Their programs were broadly committed to transcendental realism: they sought the thing-in-itself, an object whose being was not dependent upon human consciousness.

Kant's training as a student was mostly in Latin. Whatever comparatively modest Greek he knew, Plato and Aristotle are more likely than any other philosophical authors. If anything can be said simply about the status of mathematics for these writers it would be this: mathematics is not the science of that which necessarily follows from what Reason [*nous?*] has already put into the concepts; rather mathematics is the science that expresses the structure of the thing-in-itself. On the one hand, for Plato, mathematics is the dianoetic science that precisely expresses the structure of forms, while for Aristotle, on the other hand, it is a science of objective quantity. In both cases, humans believed they discovered a structure of *phusis* or Nature, a structure whose being does not depend upon us for its intelligibility. The meaning of mathematics was contained within the very traditional project that Kant explicitly recognizes when he addresses the heretofore groping of metaphysical speculations— the commitment to the search for the thing-in-itself, tied to a correspondence theory of truth and similitude theory of reference, not the a priori structure of cognition.

And if the Pythagorean ideology of mathematics was Kant's central focus—through Neoplatonic revivals—here too he could not find support for his provocative assertions. The Pythagoreans believed that they had discovered a structure in nature, not that they supposed they discovered their own a priori structure of cognition in experience. They were a religious order taken with the powerful idea that nature had an interpenetrating structure, whose interrelations could be articulated in a highly precise form, in the newly discovered language of numbers. To illustrate the case, one can simply point out that the idea of the harmony of the spheres dawned when the Pythagoreans believed they had discovered that the distances of the planets from earth bore a relation describable as 4:3, 3:2, 2:1—the musical ratios of the fifth, fourth, and octave—and thus it was supposed that these whirling heavenly bodies produced a kind of harmonic euphony. The idea presupposes a microcosmically-macrocosmically related—or interpenetrated—universe.[3] If anything, the ideal that all things are number, that numbers are real, suggests that the mind can grasp and express the intimate and complex details of nature in a language of staggering precision, an exactitude that produced tremendous monumental architecture on Pythagoras' native and contemporary Samos with the great temple of Hera and the astonishing tunnel of Eupalinos. Thus, early Greek mathematics is testimony of a commitment to transcendental—not empirical—realism. For Kant to have been right, they would have had to be empirical realists, but also transcendental idealists, like himself.

More important than noting that Kant was historically mistaken, however, is to discover how Kant was mistaken. To proclaim that a revolution in science took place when we cannot easily say when, where, or how it took place, is to cast the usefulness of such an expression into doubt. To insist that the Greek geometers made a discovery of an order that seems, historically speaking, grossly anachronistic, seems no less dubious. Even if Kant were right in assessing the Greek discovery—that contrary to their own declared understanding of envisaging an order in nature, indeed what they somehow actually achieved was the consciousness of the a priori conditions that they themselves imposed upon their constructions (and thus discovered that space and time were internal forms of consciousness?)—how would this help us better to understand either the achievement of Greek science, or moreover be better convinced about the discovery of this God's eye point of view of the structure of subjectivity?

The difficulty of assessing Kant's view of what makes for an intellectual revolution bears analogy to assessing the proposal of whether Copernicus effects a scientific revolution. If Copernicus' contemporaries failed to regard his publication of *De Revolutionibus* as revolutionary (quite independently of using the term in the political sense of radical upheaval), if the review of historical circumstances suggests that Copernicus was not supposed within his own times to effect a scientific revolution, then what illumination shall we gain by insisting that such a revolution indeed was effected whether he believed it or not? It could only be illuminating if we supposed that our assessment was an expression of a privileged point of view, a God's eye perspective. As soon as we restrain ourselves from making that demand, the desire to impose that parlance where it is inappropriate rightly dissipates.

Kant claims that there were radical upheavals that placed mathematics and natural science on the secure path of a science, just as Kuhn suggested that Copernicus had effected a revolution. But, if the evidence undermines the declared principle that a scientific revolution took place, whose adequacy is demonstrated by harmonizing the appearances—if Kant is truly a proponent of a coherence theory of truth—then what happens to the force of Kant's argument, whose illumination evidently depends upon the historical chapters that he has called upon to model for his self-proclaimed discovery? The cogent response would seem to be that, minimally, Kant must reliquish both the argument and the model, subject to redesign.

Instead, no doubt, he would insist that nothing is to be given up; but that seems so because he never regarded such historical or empirical— that is, a posteriori—chapters as significant to the degree that the rhetoric demanded in the first place. His attitude would be just the one described in the *Hamburger Correspondent* in 1804, which reported a contemporary's reflection on Kant's stubborn attitude toward his a priori claims, in this case connected with the French Revolution: "It was difficult and almost impossible to convince him that his views were wrong; even when the facts were presented against these views, he was not convinced, at least not immediately, and not always."[4] And was not the very same disposition revealed by Count Purgstall, who was generally, and more than simply, enthusiastic about Kant, and whose high praise was sobered by a realistic analysis of Kant's personality. The a priori constraints were part of Kant's parochialism, surprisingly enough. The count pointed out that Kant suffered from the dangers, faults, and imperfections of his office: "Thus, he cannot bear to hear others talk much, becomes impatient, at least for the moment, if anyone professes to know anything better than he does, monopolizes the conversation, and professes to know everything about all countries, places, divisions of the earth, and the like."[5] To illustrate to what extent this a priori science operates entirely independent of the a posteriori domain in which principles find their test of validity, whose results cannot be refuted by anything broadly experimental—and thus suggests how distorted the hypothetico-deductive method became when it finally found application to metaphysics, despite his insistence to the contrary—Count Purgstall gives several examples. "For instance, he professed to know better than I do what kind of fowls we have, how our country looks, what degree of culture our Catholic priests have attained and similar things. And this was done in spite of the fact that he had never been in the region under consideration."[6] The a priori program determines beforehand, not merely the conditions of knowability, but evidently the content to be known as well. Not only is investigation a posteriori underplayed—despite the rhetoric—but it seems increasingly dispensable. The consequence was an abrupt and rather rude distortion of the method he claimed illuminated his vision, and thus in turn, a distorted vision of the scientific revolution. All this, it seems, was a consequence of the a priori program, the securing of a God's eye point of view, tied to his insistence upon certainty, whose driving motivation was the avoidance of scepticism.

The case for Kant's assessment of the motivation of Galileo, Torricelli, and Stahl fares no better than that of the Greek mathematicians. The claim that "reason has insight only into that which it produces after a plan of its own" is the "revolution in thinking" that Kant believes to have been effected by the efforts of these thinkers. The examples, Kant modestly suggests in a footnote, make no pretense to trace "the exact course of the history of the experimental method" (Bxiii note), for already by 1787, Kant can insist that no precise knowledge of its first beginnings have become clear. But this much seems to be the case. The revolution in thinking effected in natural science can be discovered, Kant believes, by focusing upon the experimental method, for as a result of its practice, says Kant, "a light broke upon all students of nature" (Bxiii). That light proved to be, according to Kant, the discovery that Reason can have insight only into its own doings, and so what those like Galileo discovered were conditions which, imposed beforehand, were indeed nothing other than Reason's own plan, "that which it has itself put into nature." Reason, never satisfied with anything less than a binding and unifying law, could never succeed in making such a discovery if our investigations were limited to mere observation and inspection. Hence Reason, having supposed such laws—those articulated in the Analogies, the schematized categories in general—guides experimental efforts throughout in accordance with these principles that it has imposed upon experience. In trying to make sense of Kant's theory of science, and its purported revolutionary character, we are immediately called to wonder whether Galileo, Torricelli, or Stahl supposed themselves to be doing anything of the sort.

In the case of Galileo, Kant refers us to the "inclined-plane experiment": " . . . Galileo caused balls, the weights of which he had himself previously determined, to roll down an inclined plane. . . . " (Bxii).[7] There is a discussion of the motion of a ball down an inclined plane in the "First Day" of Galileo's *Dialogue Concerning Two World Systems*, a book which Kant owned.[8] There are also two references in Galileo's *Dialogues Concerning Two New Sciences*, a work with which Kant might have been familiar secondhand,[9] through references to it in Wolff's *Elementa Matheseos Universae*.[10] The issue of naturally accelerated motion is taken up in the discussion of the "Third Day." In all three cases, the conditions of the inclined-plane experiment require the motion of perfectly round and smooth balls, on a perfectly smooth plane. There is, first of all, no mention of the measurement of weight, as Kant has in mind.[11] Second, the experiment requires that all accidental impediments such as air resistance, and the like, be set aside—conditions that could not actually be re-created a posteriori. Thus, some scholars, like Gerald Holton, suggested that the "experiment" makes sense as a "thought-experiment" only, and seemed to make a trial a posteriori, indeed for Galileo, impossible.[12] Koyre argued that Galileo probably never attempted such an experiment; it was just as well, in his estimation, since the experiment could not play the clear and decisive role of proof demanded of it by Galileo.[13] Rupert Hall added support to Koyre's contention, further undercutting the possibility of performing the experiment, by noting that there were causes of experimental error that Galileo could not have evaluated, that the specific results were not applicable, independently, to free fall, and finally that Galileo relies entirely upon assertion rather than data.[14] But, within the last twenty years, that view has been largely overturned by the manuscript discoveries and ingenious re-creation by Thomas Settle.[15] It is now generally agreed among historians of science that Galileo indeed performed experiments on an inclined plane, and reached his conclusions as a result of those empirical or a posteriori demonstrations. Can these results be squared with Kant's insistence that Galileo believed he had discovered a priori presuppositions that Reason had already put into nature? It seems that that would be asking too much.

For far more likely is the case, as Hanson had suggested, that Galileo was motivated to test hypotheses in such a way that a public forum was created, the results of which sought appeal to an objectivity beyond subjective sentiment.[16] To suggest that the plan for an experiment is conceived beforehand in accordance with certain presumptions is clearly reasonable. But, to claim that either Galileo or Torricelli supposed—which Kant expressly does (Bxiii)—their undertakings to be an enterprise of discovering what they had already put into nature, is to assert a case, not argue for it, since there is apparently no evidence to that effect. The case against Kant's assessment of Galileo's intentions is furthered by considering Galileo's motivation for inventing publicly observable instruments such as a telescope, a geometrical and military compass, a pendulum regulator for clockwork, or a thermoscope.[17] Were these inventions inspired by anything except a desire to undermine merely subjective determinations that an individual might read into the consequent findings? When Torricelli, Galileo's student, developed the thermoscope into a thermometer was he not following in such a tradition, the object of which was to remove some subjective sentiment from a distinguishable and significant meaning of objective measurement? As for Stahl, the same objections apply *mutatis mutandis*, only in addition it is all the more interesting that the very example of an enlightened science that Kant brings forth was the foundation of the phlogiston theory of combustion, a novel hypothesis that ultimately proved false, undermined in the mid-1770s by Lavoisier, and of whose work Kant seems unaware.[18]

"We often find that we understand an author better than he has understood himself," so says Kant at one point in the *Critique* (A314/B370). Perhaps Kant is telling us something that these great thinkers did not know about their own discoveries and intentions, as unusual a technique as it may be in the history of science. But it is difficult to accept that some "Thales," who is customarily credited with breaking away from mythological explanation by recognizing and advancing the very possibility of naturalistic explanation, or a Galileo proceeded as if they imagined their discoveries were self-imposed conditions of Reason. The experimental character of their efforts cannot, on Kant's view, claim to be an appeal to experience—a posteriori—in any significant sense, for the advance in mathematics that also makes such an "experiment" (*Versuch*) is a construction in pure intuition alone. Thus despite Kant's claims—that (a) "we cannot, in general . . . anticipate general natural science" (A171/B213), and that (b) "Special laws, as concerning those appearances which are empirically determined, cannot in their specific character be derived from the categories . . . " (B165), and hence require an appeal to experience, the central assumption that predominated was that (c) all those special laws "are one and all subject to them [categories]" (B165). The appeal to experience amounts to nothing more than a determination of the specific conditions under which the categories hold, the specific determinations under which we generally impose conditions upon experience. The rhetoric declares that specific scientific laws must be discovered a posteriori, but the focus of Kant's attention was upon the a priori character that guaranteed certainty. Already in the A edition of the "Transcendental Deduction," Kant had further revealed this troubling ambiguity when he attempted to make his position on the nature of science clear: "However exaggerated and absurd it may sound, to say that the understanding is itself the source of the laws of nature . . . such an assertion is nonetheless correct" (A127).

The revolution in philosophy that Kant hopes to effect, on the order of Newton's demonstration, reflects his strategy that if he can account for that fundamental discovery that placed various human enterprises—logic, mathematics, natural science—on *der sichere Gang einer Wissenschaft*,[19] he can, employing that singular model applicable to all three cases, achieve comparable success for metaphysics. What happens to Kant's argument if the historical exegesis of the discoveries in mathematics and natural science are unsound because unsupportable based upon historical complexities that escaped his notice? That argument collapses. And what happens when we find ourselves with a conceptual inheritance of a scientific revolution embedded within these Kantian origins? We must consider discarding this infelicitous legacy.

CHAPTER 4

A Brief Survey of the Secondary Literature on the Expression "Kant's Copernican Revolution"

Kant spoke of himself as effecting a "Copernican Revolution" in Philosophy.

—Bertrand Russell (1948)

Kant claimed that he had effected a "Copernican Revolution" in Philosophy.

—John Dewey (1929)

. . . an idea which Kant himself proudly calls his "Copernican Revolution."

—Karl Popper (1962)

This subjectivity means nothing but what Kant's "Copernican Revolution" implies.

—Ernst Cassirer (1918)

Kant called his innovation in the realm of knowledge a "Copernican Revolution."

—Karl Jaspers (1957)[1]

IMPORTANT PHILOSOPHERS WITH WIDE INFLUENCE, LIKE RUSSELL, DEWEY, Popper, Cassirer, and Jaspers, have claimed that Kant effected a Copernican revolution in philosophy.[2] Kant specialists of no less rank than Kemp Smith, Paton, Ewing, Weldon, Beck, Körner, Strawson, Wilkerson, Broad, Brittain, Melnick, Pippin, and Scruton, among others, have all acknowledged that Kant believed himself to be effecting a Copernican revolution in philosophy. Could all of these thinkers have been wrong about what Kant said or believed he said? As surprising as it must seem, certainly to this writer, they were all mistaken in this respect. Kant never describes the revolution that he seeks to effect as a Copernican revolution. We have already considered the deficiencies in that mistaken analogy in sufficient detail. It is simply worth restating that the error is not simply a verbal quibble. The error reveals a supposition about the suitability of applying terms like "revolution" (as radical upheaval) to Copernicus—and his *De Revolutionibus*—whose meaning was quite different, and whose contemporaries never came to view his work as radical in that required sense. Attributing this self-proclaimed Copernican revolution to Kant not only misrepresents his expressed opinion on the matter, but it distorts the structure of science as he understood it, and hence the conditions that made possible the revolution in science, and thus the model on whose analogy Kant sought to illuminate and construct the definitive science of metaphysics. In this brief chapter, first evidence is presented to show how widespread and deeply entrenched in the secondary literature is the perception that Kant effected a Copernican revolution in philosophy; then, the text is examined to clarify precisely what Kant said.

In the first edition of the *Critique of Pure Reason*, 1781, there is not a single mention of Copernicus by name; in the revised, second edition, there are two references to Copernicus, both contained in the Preface.[3] The references to Copernicus have produced highly differing reactions from commentators. Some have taken the metaphor to be instructive and significant, and have gone so far as to refer to Kant's whole critical enterprise as a Copernican revolution in philosophy; transforming the prevailing and traditional programs in metaphysics, by reversing the order of inquiry, Kant sought—not the conditions under which the mind conforms to objects, but rather—the conditions under which an object conforms to the mind. Other commentators have suggested that the metaphor is misleading or entirely wrongheaded; for although Copernicus might indeed have discovered a fruitful theoretical approach to the motions of the heavenly bodies by relying upon the spectator's or knower's role in the act of observation, Copernicus effectively displaced the knower from the center of the world when, heliocentrically, he placed not only the earth in motion but removed it from the center of the heavens. These critics maintained that Kant's epistemology, insisting upon the conformity of object to the knower, propounds an anthropocentric model, while Copernicus, for whatever other similarities might be detected, effectively undermines the anthropocentric project. A third distinguishable group of scholars such as Friedrich, Hanson, Engel, Findlay, Ameriks, and most recently I. Bernard Cohen, have pointed out that Kant never asserted such a thing, or carefully steer clear of employing this locution, but this still leaves open the question of what sense Kant had in mind when he attempts to illuminate his project by some sort of analogy with Copernicus' thought. I turn to survey the field of secondary literature to clarify this situation.

Kant's theory of knowledge, set out in the *Critique of Pure Reason*, has often been described as a Copernican revolution in philosophy. In the Introduction to the 1981 edition of the translation of Cassirer's *Kant's Life and Thought*, Körner focuses upon Kant's Copernican revolution in philosophy, describes it as an entirely new conception of philosophy and philosophical method, and declares it to initiate two new kinds of questions, one "of fact" (*quid facti*), and the other "of legality" (*quid jurus*).[4] Cassirer himself says Kant's Copernican revolution "signifies the result not of the object but of a specific lawfulness of cognition, to which a determinate form of objectivity is to be traced back."[5] Brittan suggested, in 1978, that Kant's Copernican revolution amounted to a philosophical program whose main thrust was the rejection of reductionism.[6] Pippin in 1982, offered that "[Kant] argues for a Copernican Revolution in philosophy, a transcendental turn to issues of prior importance in methodological terms than had been appreciated by much of the tradition."[7] Scruton, also in 1982, claimed that the essence of Kant's Copernican revolution in philosophy was an understanding of the peculiar kind of self-consciousness that required that the world conform to certain conditions that we impose upon it.[8] In 1984, Beck reflected upon Kant's Copernican revolution in philosophy, declaring that "The knowing subject can understand any phenomenon of the world (whether or not it involves motion) only if he takes account of his own contribution. . . ."[9] In the 1984 translation of Deleuze's work, Kant's Copernican revolution arises as a rejection of dogmatic rationalism; "the *necessary* submission of object to subject replaced the prevailing *harmony* between subject and object"; "the essential discovery," according to Deleuze, was that "the faculty of knowledge is *legislative*."[10] Earlier, in 1966, Strawson had described the essence of Kant's Copernican revolution as "the theory of the mind making Nature."[11] Wilkerson, in 1976, followed Strawson's lead, characterizing Kant's Copernican revolution in philosophy as the effort to make "the phenomenal world dependent upon our own cognitive apparatus, since it is only that way that we can guarantee a priori knowledge of objects."[12] Broad envisages Kant's revolution to run parallel to the astronomical innovation of Copernicus in terms of a transformation in method when he declared, in 1978, "We can now understand what Kant means when he claims to have made a revolution in philosophy like that which Copernicus made in astronomy."[13] Melnick, in 1973, suggested that Kant's Copernican revolution is to reinterpret the question

"What is an object?" to ask instead "How does the experience of some subject connect up to his judgmental apparatus?" and so focuses upon the judging subject.[14] In all these cases, three things become clear: (i) the expression "Kant's Copernican revolution in philosophy" is supposed to be significant and informative, (ii) despite some resemblances, there is, granting its significance, surprisingly little consensus among commentators as to its precise meaning, and (iii) the minimal family resemblance in these assessments consists in an understanding of the change in method, procedure, or generally point of view, which forced a reinterpretation of the prevailing philosophical programs. They express the recognition that the expression "Copernican revolution" indicates a feature both of Kant's project in metaphysics as well as his appraisal of the structure of science with which it intersects: the intersection is the a priori dimension of the enterprises. The error committed by all these thinkers is to confuse the transformation in method, which for Kant represents a novel *hypothesis*, with a sufficient condition for establishing the revolutionary character of a science. For until the rigorous deduction is presented, there is no way to distinguish, in Kant's own estimation, the indispensable hypothesis for scientific advance from the wild and ridiculous metaphysical hypothesis that he so adamantly rejected.

The tradition that discusses Kant's Copernican revolution in philosophy extends back into the nineteenth century where the debate focused upon the potentially misleading and wrongheaded aspects of Kant's metaphor. In the writings of Green[15] and Stirling,[16] for example, the content specific to the astronomical analogy was supposed to be significant; Lange[17] and Hoffding[18] followed similarly, supposing part of the significance of Kant's philosophy to consist in an embracing of particular astronomical tenets. Samuel Alexander, writing in 1909, discussed Kant's Copernican revolution but complained that, quite to the contrary, Kant's philosophy is itself both Ptolemaic and anthropocentric in character.[19] The same sort of criticism was put forth by Bertrand Russell: "Kant spoke of himself as having effected a 'Copernican revolution', but he would have been more accurate if he had spoken of a 'Ptolemaic counter-revolution,' since he put Man back at the centre from which Copernicus had de-throned him."[20] Kemp Smith[21] follows Watson,[22] in opposition to those like Green and Alexander, arguing that the specific astronomical content was irrelevant to the analogy.[23] Kant's point, according to Kemp Smith was that as "the spectator projects his own motions into the heavens; [so] human reason legislates for the domain of natural science. The sphere of fixed stars is proved to be motionless; things in themselves are freed from the limitations of space and time."[24] Following Kemp Smith, reacting against a view which supposed astronomical detail to be significant to—and thereby misleading in—Kant's analogy, Paton, in 1936, insisted that Kant compared his own philosophical revolution to that initiated by Copernicus.[25] In 1938, Ewing agreed, and further suggested that Kant supposed he resembled Copernicus in attributing to ourselves what his predecessors had attributed to reality.[26] Kemp Smith, Paton, and Ewing, responding to those like Green and Alexander, were compelled to treat the astronomical content as instructive, instead of merely insisting upon the methodological similarities. Thus, even if we suppose that there is some analogy between Kant's enterprise, as he sees it, and that undertaken by Copernicus, it is still not clear just what that analogy is.

In 1949, Friedrich refers, not to Kant's Copernican revolution, but speaks only of "the first thought of Copernicus."[27] In 1959, Hanson followed suit; he specifically objected to attributing to Kant this label that he never claimed.[28] In 1963, Engel did likewise.[29] More recently, in 1981, Findlay discussed the "Copernican view,"[30] and in 1982, Ameriks cautiously speaks of Kant's "Copernican image" of philosophy.[31] A far cry from Swing's 1969 declaration that "Kant called his doctrine of a priori cognition the Copernican Revolution in Metaphysics,"[32] there is no mention anywhere in the surviving corpus, nonetheless the *Critique of Pure Reason*, of a Copernican revolution. It is now time to reexamine precisely what Kant does say, and to clarify the analogy that Kant does make between himself and Copernicus.

In a passage in the Preface to the B edition, where the expression "revolution" appears six times (Bxi–xxiv), especially in the phrase "*Revolution der Denkart*," in the text, Kant refers to Copernicus for the first time. The expression he uses is *den ersten Gedanken des Kopernikus* ("the first thought of Copernicus"). In order to understand what Kant has in mind, this expression must be reset within the argument advanced.

The argument begins in a new paragraph that opens at Bxvi. First, Kant acknowledges that both mathematics and natural science achieved their secure status as sciences by a "single" and "sudden" "revolution." These remarkable results encouraged Kant to consider the fundamental feature in the changed point of view by virtue of which they established themselves. Their success Kant regards as a sufficient reason to at least try to imitate, insofar as such an innovation can be accommodated, in metaphysics the change in point of view that led the way to effecting that revolution. Then, Kant simply acknowledges the prevailing point of view in metaphysics that in his estimation has led nowhere, namely the supposition that our knowledge must conform to objects—the correspondence theory of knowledge together with the similitude theory of reference. As Kant will explain a few sentences later, this approach could not provide the requisite certainty that is a necessary feature of a science. For so long as our knowledge corresponds to objects, our knowledge is at best a series of probable generalizations from the contents of sensation—the empiricist program—and the catastrophic and unpalatable consequence of accepting that point of view is the inescapability of scepticism.

The change in point of view he will now advance requires that the prospect of certainty is first secured: our knowledge must be a priori, and the empiricist program can never attain that infallible status. The proposed change in point of view, in the attempt to imitate the success of natural science, leads him to wonder about the consequences if we supposed that the method of inquiry were somehow reversed by insisting that objects correspond to our knowledge—the coherence theory of truth together with the rejection of a similitude theory of reference. Kant pursues this change in point of view because the prospect of certainty is at least possible if we employ this new method. Now comes the use in question: "We should then be proceeding precisely along the lines of the first thought of Copernicus. Failing of satisfactory progress in explaining the movements of the heavenly bodies on the supposition that they all revolved around the spectator, he tried whether he might not have better success if he made the spectator revolve and the stars remain at rest" (Bxvi). It is on analogy with this transformation in point of view that he calls upon Copernicus, and seeks to imitate his efforts so far as he understood them.

He then proposes to make an "experiment" (equals thought-experiment) in metaphysics on that analogy, and emphasizes the crucial point, again: "If intuition must conform to the constitution of objects [the point of view of traditional metaphysics], I do not see how we could know anything of the latter a priori; but if the object . . . must conform to the constitution of our faculty of intuition, I have no difficulty in conceiving such a possibility" (Bxvii). Copernicus, for Kant, provides a novel hypothesis in terms of a changed point of view that he supposed led to the effecting of a revolution in natural science. To effect a revolution a rigorous deduction must be provided, and there is absolutely no evidence that Kant envisioned Copernicus in that light. Thus, Copernicus, for Kant, is not merely the proponent of a novel hypothesis, but an hypothesis that so happened eventually led to proofs that transformed the enterprise of natural science. To make clear that this is explicitly what

Copernicus meant to Kant when he wrote the B Preface, we can turn to the second and last reference to Copernicus where these suspicions are further corroborated.

In a footnote to Bxxii, Kant also refers to Copernicus while making two points, first with reference to the status of an hypothesis ultimately proved by the articulation of the fundamental laws of motion, and second with a comment on method whereby Copernicus dared to assert what was contradictory to the senses, but nonetheless true, in seeking the observed movements not in the heavenly bodies but in the spectators. First, it was "the fundamental laws of the motions of the heavenly bodies which gave established certainty to what Copernicus assumed only as an hypothesis" (Bxxii, note). As I shall show in Chapter 6, following the officially sanctioned account in Wolff's *Elementa Matheseos Universae*, the fundamental laws of motion are sometimes supposed to be supplied by Kepler (and other times by Newton), and this might suggest the appropriateness of referring to Kant's proposed revolution as a Keplerian revolution in philosophy. This is not a bad suggestion. But, the complete or wider system that makes intelligible Kepler's efforts was provided by Newton's deduction of the principle of attraction—the universal gravitation that "holds the universe together" (Bxxii, note). This is how Wolff understands the perspective on demonstration, and I shall argue that it is broadly within this context that Kant understands the scientific revolution. Newton gave established certainty to what Copernicus advanced as a mere hypothesis.

The crucial point is that, having accepted the hypothetico-deductive method as a model that he seeks to accomodate to and construct upon a science of metaphysics, Copernicus represents the proponents of novel hypotheses but not of deductions. Intellectual revolutions are heralded by the rigorous deductions. Thus, it is precisely for this reason that it is mistaken to identify Kant's *Critique* with a Copernican revolution because the hypothesis, without the deduction, although indispensable, cannot in and of itself be distinguished from the wild and ridiculous hypotheses that Kant rails against, which also have no rigorous deduction (and never shall). I shall consider the equivocal use which Kant makes of the term "hypothesis" in Chapter 5. Thus, the consequence of mistakingly attributing a Copernican revolution to Kant is to misrepresent the method of demonstration that Kant adopts as the very *modus operandi* of the critical philosophy.

Thus, following this analogy, Kant seeks to imitate Copernicus' *Umänderung der Denkart* by sharing the spectator's or knower's point of view: when accommodated to metaphysics, Kant's transformation means that objects must conform to the conditions of cognition, which we bring to and impose upon experience a priori. But, what he has shared with Copernicus is merely the suggestion of a novel hypothesis, and thus, in his own terms, no revolution at all. He insists that this change in point of view, on analogy with Copernicus, is an hypothesis only, advanced merely "in order to draw attention to the character of these first attempts at such a change" (Bxxii, note). In and of themselves alone, such hypotheses are not enough. Thus, "in the *Critique* itself," he insists, "it [equals the sufficiency of the hypothesis of such a change in point of view] will be proved, apodeictically not hypothetically. . ." (Bxxii, note).

In addition to these references to Copernicus by name I have found only two other mentions relating Copernican ideology. In the first *Critique*, the "Copernican system" is mentioned *(dem kopernikanischen Weltsystem*, A257/B313), in a garbled passage, in which the Copernican system is allied with theoretical astronomy, as opposed to observational astronomy. Some eleven years later, in the *Contest of the Faculties* (1798), Kant employs the expression the "Copernican Hypothesis" (*kopernikanischen Hypothese*) in the context of discussing the age-old question of whether or not the human race is constantly progressing.

In that passage from the second part of the *Contest of the Faculties*, Kant is contrasting theoretical knowledge with practical knowledge. In astronomy—Kant means theoretical knowledge in general—we can discover a privileged point of view; not so with free actions. If we suppose, following "Copernicus' Hypothesis," that the sun is the focus of the planetary orbits, the constant motions of the planets follow a regular course. The discovery of this privileged point of view is "an act which only reason can perform" precisely because we are forced to abandon common sense as a guide in theoretical knowledge. Thus, Copernicus still represents for Kant, more than a decade after the B Preface, the formulator of a novel *hypothesis* only.[33] Granting both the supposed significance of Copernicus' contribution to Kant's critical philosophy, and the very restricted occasions on which he felt inclined to mention him, the matter deserves deeper examination. In doing so, the intention is to gain clarification into Kant's project, which so many commentators have found useful to investigate under the rubric of a Copernican revolution in philosophy, and at the same time, reflect upon the role of Copernicus in the so-called scientific revolution so far as Kant envisaged that enterprise and Copernicus' contribution to it. I now turn to examine briefly Kant's ambiguous use of the term "hypothesis" in order to clarify further his understanding of the hypothetico-deductive method.

CHAPTER 5

Kant's Revolution and the Ambiguous Use of Hypotheses

IN THE PREFACE TO THE B EDITION OF THE *CRITIQUE* OF 1787, KANT RECOGnizes the indispensability of hypotheses; he credits Copernicus with formulating an hypothesis without which the fundamental laws of motion and the principle of universal gravitation would have remained forever undiscovered. In the Preface to the A edition six years earlier, Kant insisted that any claims bearing even the slightest resemblance to an hypothesis were to be treated as contraband, an illegal substance prohibited by law; he insisted that any such claim was to be immediately confiscated and not put up for sale even at the lowest price. On the one hand, it seems that hypotheses are indispensable to the very method of science on which he models his metaphysics; on the other hand, he regards them as unacceptable and entirely impermissible. How shall we reconcile these apparently conflicting views?

The apparent conflict can be resolved by the time-honored device of making different uses of the term "hypotheses" refer to different offices. Reason employs hypotheses$_1$ in science in a regulative or programmatic manner in carrying out its legislative functions while attempting to determine the course of nature; Reason employs hypotheses$_2$ in metaphysical speculations in a polemical manner that has a dialectical value, at best, in calling Reason to its own inherent limitations and thereby restraint. Hypotheses$_1$ are indispensable to scientific progress, and thereby are to be countenanced. Hypotheses$_2$, while at most revealing the peculiar fate that Reason is burdened by questions by its own nature that it cannot ignore and yet that transcending its powers it cannot answer, are impermissible admissions in the *Critique* in whose domain only the certain need apply. The apparent conflict is just that—only apparent; Kant uses the term equivocally, and by distinguishing those different uses, the tension can be greatly, if not entirely, resolved. As Kemp Smith told the awful truth more than half a century ago: ". . . Kant flatly contradicts himself in almost every chapter; and there is hardly a technical term which is not employed by him in a variety of different and conflicting senses."[1] It would, I think, be asking too much to suggest that all ambiguity can be resolved in the case of "hypotheses," "revolution," or most any another significant term in his work.

Almost a quarter-century ago, Robert Butts discussed the complex and ambiguous uses of the term "hypothesis" in Kant's writings.[2] He believed that at least four senses could be isolated: (1) the programmatic or regulative sense in science, (2) the polemical use of transcendental hypotheses, whose force he compares with Rescher's belief-contravening suppositions, (3) those with a practical bearing, employed in the ethical writings, and (4) scientific guesses about the course of nature.[3] In his impressive articles, Butts' treatment of Kantian hypotheses goes far beyond the more restricted issue I have taken up here, most especially the treatment in the *Logik*. The task with which I am concerned is clarifying what Copernicus meant to Kant; in this regard, the hypothesis promulgated by Copernicus, in Kant's estimation, seems to bring together both (1) and (4) in Butts' classification: the Copernican hypothesis both programmatically or regulatively guides research, and at the same time presents a guess about the course of nature.[4] Accordingly, both of those senses are expressed in what I am calling Kant's use of hypotheses$_1$. That use I want to distinguish from the A Preface-talk that pronounces hypotheses to be anathema, and which I am calling hypotheses$_2$.

Insofar as Kant wants to distinguish sharply (a) natural science from (b) traditional speculative metaphysics, the twofold division of hypotheses seems adequate to separate further those enterprises. The use of hypotheses$_1$ is methodologically necessary for the progress of the sciences; hypotheses$_2$, even if polemically expedient, however, is the troubling employment that Kant seeks to disengage and disenfranchise from positive science. But, even adopting this analysis, a central point remains undisclosed. How shall we determine the difference between these two kinds of hypotheses? Of course, it shall be granted that the minimal conditions for accepting any statement must be met by any hypothesis—in the first and approbative sense. The minimal condition is that the statement, treated conditionally, refers to a possible object of experience. Thus, two criteria must be met, both of which can best be stated negatively: (i) the hypothesis cannot violate the principle of contradiction—logical necessity, and (ii) the hypothesis cannot violate the synthetic a priori principles—categorial necessity. But, granting these conditions, the difference between hypotheses$_1$ and hypotheses$_2$ has not been secured. In that difference consists the accolade for Copernicus and the ridicule for the dogmatic metaphysicians.

The sense of hypotheses that Butts seems to have missed is the one discussed by Wolff in his treatise on scientific method, appended to the
Elementa Mechanicae, which Kant taught in 1759 and 1760, and which I
shall discuss in detail in the next chapter. For the time being, I shall emphasize that view, which adds an additional ambiguity, but which helps to clarify how Kant understands Copernicus. Kant was concerned, following
Wolff, not merely with the wild and ridiculous dogmatic hypotheses but
also with the outlandish hypotheses advanced by those engaging in scientific activity, which could only depreciate the discipline in general. An hypothesis which lacks proof—although perhaps indispensable to scientific
progress—cannot really be countenanced, since it is in principle indistin-
guishable from the wild and ridiculous hypotheses that also lack proof.
It was the definitive proof—the deduction—which provided the valid demonstration, which in turn elevated a statement to the status of an hypothesis that could indeed be countenanced.

Wolff makes his point by insisting that although hypotheses are indispensable, that without their employment there would be no hope of uncovering the truth—just as Kant declares that Newton's achievement would
have forever remained undiscovered were it not for Copernicus'
hypothesis—authors must nevertheless abstain from publishing, that is,
publically declaring, their hypotheses until they are definitively proved.
The reason he offers is that this is the only way to avoid the problem of undermining confidence in the soundness of the scientific enterprise by circulating figments of the imagination. Thus, Wolff understands that the
thinker who pursues the study of natural science runs precisely the same
risk of casting the discipline into ridicule by the publication of unproven
hypotheses—however sound they may turn out to be—as the dogmatic
metaphysicians who publicly spread wild and unprovable hypotheses.
Without the definitive proof, both kinds of hypotheses share the same infelicitous status. I quote the Latin passage:

> . . . quomodo in investigandis veritatibus a posteriori sit procedendum &
> quam indispensabilis usus sit hypothesium, ut si iisdem uti nolueris, nulla
> supersit spes veritatis unquam detegendae. . . . Non est quod excipias
> hypothesibus equidem locum esse concedendum in inveniendo, ab iis tamen
> esse abstinendum in libris, qui publici juris fiunt. Entenim ubi veritates ab
> iis, quae nobis perspecta sunt, principiis procul remotae sunt, ut a priori
> denegatur add eas accessus.[5]

It is worth emphasizing again, in light of this passage, that to identify
Kant's proposed revolution in philosophy with a Copernican revolution
is to misunderstand the structure of the scientific method on which he mod-

els his critique of metaphysics. Copernicus' hypothesis, without the required and definitive proof that Kant in no way believes he provides, cannot claim—in Wolffian-Kantian terms—the right to be set aside from the most outlandish dogmatic fantasies. This is why, it seems to me, Kant is so entirely unwilling to countenance any hypotheses in his A Preface, and it is only because of the subsequent definitive deduction by Kepler and Newton that he will countenance Copernicus in the B Preface.

I now turn briefly to review the argument of the A Preface to clarify the context of the dismissal of all hypotheses, and at the same time show how in 1781 Kant already thought of science and metaphysics in terms of a political analogy. In 1781, Kant was prepared only to attempt to "restore" metaphysics to the dignified status from which it had fallen, and only after "reform." Within more or less half a decade, he changes his political strategy, and in the B Preface will call for a "revolution" and steps forward as its leader.

Although the term "revolution" does not appear in the A edition of 1781, Kant expressly believed that his *Critique* produced a fundamental transformation in point of view in metaphysics. On 11 May 1781, Kant writes, "My book can produce nothing other than a total change in outlook in this area of human knowledge. . . . What I am working on in the *Critique* is not metaphysics [sc. in the traditional sense] but a totally new and hitherto unattempted science. . . ."[6] In the Preface to the A edition, the state of metaphysical pursuits is expressed in terms of a political analogy, and it is the dethroned monarch—"Metaphysics," "Queen of all the sciences" (Aviii)—which Kant sets out to restore. In the language of 1781, he contents himself to enact "reform and restoration" (Ax) on "her government" (Aix), rather than "revolution." By 1787, he changes his political strategy; then he decides that reform and restoration are insufficient. Instead, he will not merely sanction but lead the revolution, and will install himself as the new sovereign, following the tribunal in which, as the voice of Reason, he will serve as judge. Not unlike Socrates who in Plato's *Apology* will examine and judge the jury about what the jury supposedly knows best—justice, Kant will lead the revolution of Reason, judge the battle, and rather than restore the matronly queen of the sciences, will assume the sovereignty himself by enacting the legislative and judicial functions of Reason.

In 1781, Kant attempts to illuminate the sorry state of metaphysics by use of a political analogy. The analogy asks us to consider the conditions under which legitimate authority is undermined. On that analogy, Kant seeks a restoration of that legitimate authority, but only after reform. As the monarch legislates, so does Reason. The danger to the monarch, however, is found in the barbarism of intestine wars that challenge her authority when she becomes despotic, and thus gives rise to anarchy; the danger to metaphysics came first from the dogmatists whose rule was despotic, and then from a new challenge from "a species of nomads" whom Kant identifies as the "sceptics" (Aix). Kant finds himself able to report the state of intestine wars in the philosophical domain. The empiricists—and hence ultimately sceptics, in Kant's estimation—like Locke, have sought to undermine Queen Metaphysics by tracing her genealogy, quite fictitiously, to vulgar origins in common experience (Aix). But, the state of that assault has been repelled; the rationalists have come to the defense of the queen, but unfortunately with "time-worn dogmatism" (Ax). On that analogy, the queen has been restored but without the needed reform, leaving the government in the same infelicitous condition.

Kant declares that his *Critique of Pure Reason* is a "tribunal" that will assure to Reason its lawful claims, not by despotic decrees but by its own eternal and unalterable laws (Axi–xii). He insists that "In this inquiry I have made completeness my chief aim, and I venture to assert that there is not a single metaphysical problem which has not been solved"(Axiii). To achieve such a result, "certainty" is an essential requirement. So important is it that he prescribes to himself the maxim in this investigation to hold no "opinions" (Axv). The impermissibility of holding opinions, the securing of certainty, is clarified by Kant's insistence on dismissing and refusing to consider all hypotheses, a point he makes, once again, by calling forth the same political metaphor. "Everything, therefore, which bears any manner of resemblance to an hypothesis is to be treated as contraband; it is not to be put up for sale even at the lowest price, but forthwith confiscated, immediately upon detection" (Axv). The reason, for Kant, is clear. The knowledge that his efforts attempt to secure is a priori, and "thus lays claim to be regarded as absolutely necessary" (Bxv). Hypotheses, at best, can only claim "conditional necessity" and therefore, Kant believes, can have no place in his *Critique*. No matter how approbative a connotation has the ambiguously employed term '*Hypotheses*' in Kant's *Critique*, it can never extricate itself from the charge of a conditional necessity that Kant found insufficient to guarantee the required certainty that the science sought to secure. Since Kant, in the B edition explicitly identifies Copernicus as the proponent of an hypothesis, the revolution in metaphysics that Kant proposes cannot be properly characterized in terms of Copernicus' achievement.

CHAPTER 6

Kant, Copernicus, and the
Copernican Revolution in Philosophy

KANT'S VIEW OF A SCIENTIFIC METHOD THAT ACCOUNTED FOR THE REMARK-
able development of scientific knowledge was not original. He inherited
that view perhaps from several sources but principal among them was
Christian von Wolff. Kant's view of Copernicus was inherited at the
same time that he inherited the general view about the growth of scientific knowledge, for the exemplary case of the successful employment of
scientific method—in Wolff's exegesis—involved the connection of Copernicus with Kepler and Newton. Although Wolff does not use the word
"revolution" to describe the growth of scientific knowledge, he indeed supposes the advance of the sciences to have achieved a radical break from
previous enterprises. What Kant does in the B Preface is to reproduce
Wolff's expressed point of view in almost the exact terms he states it,
and clearly in the same spirit. Kant declares that the use of just this
method had effected a revolution in science. Thus, except for the technical term to describe it, Kant inherits his understanding of a scientific revolution from Wolff, with regard to both method and Copernican
example. The only point he omits is the acknowledgment of Wolff as his
explicit source.

"Kant must have had first-hand acquaintance with Copernicus' *De Revolutionibus . . .* "[1] So writes Kemp Smith in his magisterial *Commentary
to Kant's "Critique of Pure Reason."* Indeed, Kant may well have, but I
am supposing that he did not, and there appears to be no evidence that
he did. Copernicus is mentioned by name only a few times in the entire corpus. Kant has very little to say about Copernicus. Even in the *Metaphysical Foundations of Natural Science* (1786), there appears not to be a
single reference to Copernicus or the Copernican system. In exploring
the possibilities for the source(s) that perhaps Kant had in mind, when
he calls upon Copernicus, I am supposing that it was Christian von
Wolff. When Kant refers twice to Copernicus in the B Preface, he is recall-
ing the treatment of Copernicus as it was presented in Wolff's *Elementa*

Matheseos Universae, a copy of which Kant owned, and which he used to teach a course on mechanics in 1759 and 1760.[2]

The difficult circumstance of gaining access to books is vastly compounded in the eighteenth-century Königsberg from which Kant hails. When Frederick the Great visited Königsberg as crown prince in 1739, he described it as "better suited to the training of bears than to becoming a theater of the sciences."[3] We should not be surprised to discover that with less than a dozen full-time faculty, in a community long sunk into provincial obscurity, the available library was hopelessly incomplete.

6.A. Kant and Copernicus: The Idea of a Novel Hypothesis

When Kant's few references to Copernicus are made explicit against the background of what precisely Copernicus says in his *De Revolutionibus*, two points become even clearer: (1) Kant could not have supposed that Copernicus effected a revolution in his own terms, and (2) Copernicus nowhere describes his own work as revolutionary, but rather envisages his efforts in a reactionary way, attempting to return to a lost but ancient wisdom. First, the references to Copernicus are briefly but explicitly summarized, and then the key passage from Copernicus' work is presented in contrast. When that has been accomplished, the case for the Wolffian source of Kant's position can be taken up in the following section, 6.B.

Kant never speaks of his enterprise as a Copernican revolution in philosophy; Kant refers to Copernicus as the proponent of a novel hypothesis. In the Bxvi passage, Kant envisages an analogy with Copernicus as effecting an *Umänderung der Denkart*, a transformation in point of view, seeking to explain phenomena, not by an accounting of the phenomena themselves but rather an accounting of the conditions imposed by the spectator/knower. In the footnote to Bxxii, Kant repeats the comparison as yielding an *Umänderung der Denkart*, a change in point of view, this time (a) contrary to common sense, and (b) accounting for observations, not by an appeal to the things observed but by appeal to the spectator/knower.

In the Bxvi passage, the proposed *Umänderung der Denkart*, is just this: rather than suppose "that all our knowledge conforms to objects. . . . we must therefore make trial [*Versuche*] whether we might not have more success in the tasks of metaphysics, if we suppose that objects must conform to our knowledge" (Bxvi). To undertake such a trans-

formation in point of view would be to proceed along the lines mit den ersten Gedanken des Kopernikus. For earlier astronomers, and perhaps Copernicus himself, had initially supposed that the heavenly bodies moved, and the earth remained at rest. Certainly, this is how it appeared—and how it appears—to a spectator on the earth; this is common sense. Failing satisfactory progress, Kant says that Copernicus "tried [*versuchte*] whether he might not have better success if he made the spectator revolve and the stars remain at rest" (Bxvi–xvii). It is this hypothesis that was "contrary to common-sense." Copernicus made a trial of something; in Kant's parlance, he employed the central methodological technique of a science, that is, he made an experiment, which could here only mean that he introduced a novel hypothesis.

From these passages, are we to suppose that Kant believed Copernicus succeeded where the earlier efforts failed? And if Kant supposes Copernicus succeeded, in what respect(s)? What would it mean, to Kant, to say that Copernicus succeeded in explaining—where others had failed—the movements of the heavenly bodies? Did the proposals of *De Revolutionibus* predict more accurately than those of Ptolemy's *Almagest* the positions or motions of the heavenly bodies? The simple answer is no.[5] If Kant supposed it did, he would have been wrong. But, it seems more likely that he did not have this sort of interpretation in mind. As the footnote to Bxxii instructs, Kant supposes Copernicus to be the proponent of an hypothesis, definitively proved only by the demonstration of the laws of motion; without that proof, Copernicus' work remains mere hypothesis. But, the hypothesis of Copernicus, in turn, was the indispensable ingredient without which, Kant suggests, Newton's own invisible force that holds the whole universe together (i.e., universal gravitation) would have remained forever undiscovered.

Copernicus, by his own work alone, did not succeed in explaining the motions of heavenly bodies—in Kant's own terms—but insofar as he provided the stepping-stone for Newton's proof, Copernicus did in fact succeed where Ptolemy had failed, and that was Copernicus' "experiment" or "trial," namely, the novel hypothesis of heliocentricity. From this hypothesis, Copernicus was not only able to advance a model accounting for celestial phenomena at least as accurate as that of Ptolemy, but did so in such as way as to (i) eliminate the "annual component"—an unexplained mirroring of the sun's motion—that Ptolemy required.[6] From the heliocentric hypothesis, a (ii) definite ordering of the planets was proposed, based upon their increasing sidereal periods from the sun, and this "ordering" was determined by means of (iii) a common measure—the earth-sun radius—which offered a means of calculating the distances of the planets from the center of the universe. In this sense, the hypothesis led to the formulation of (iv) an absolute and fixed unit of reference.[7] All these constructive advances—even if Kant understood it in this fashion—amount to mere hypotheses short of the rigorous deduction of the laws of motion. Copernicus' achievements could not be considered revolutionary in Kant's own terms.

Nor does Copernicus describe his own work as a revolution in any respect. Rather, in *De Revolutionibus*, his approach is explicitly reactionary. He envisages his enterprise in the Preface, which he dedicates to Pope Paul III, as one carrying on in the tradition of the ancients, which had gone astray. Copernicus compliments the "wonderful care and industry" of Ptolemy, but sought the return to the path set out by the ancient Greeks.[8] In that Preface, Copernicus claims that he first found mention of the hypothesis of earth's mobility in Cicero, who attributed the doctriine of Nicetas. He then acknowledges that he found more references in Plutarch, this time to the Pythagoreans like Philolaus, Heracleides of Pontus, and Ekphantus. So important did he regard this strategy of returning to the earlier pristine wisdom that he quotes that passage from Plutarch's *De placitis philosophorum* (III, 13) in that dedicatory Preface, the only such quotation to be found in that section of his work. Copernicus' declared strategy is reactionary, not revolutionary (in the modern sense of the word).

Westman showed that, except for his impassioned disciple Rheticus, Copernicus was hardly perceived as a revolutionary: "In the prevalent mood of reform, Copernicus was perceived not as a revolutionary but as a moderate reformer (like Melanchthon), returning to an ancient, pristine wisdom before Ptolemy."[9] If Kant supposed his work was revolutionary, the tone of Copernicus' work would not supply grounds for much enthusiasm. At the close of the introduction to Book 1, which occupies a mere page and a half of text, Copernicus again reminds us of his reactionary strategy, attempting to reconnect his contemporary world with the ancient wisdom, rejoining that ancient road or highway to knowledge. He concludes that introduction, ". . . I confess that I shall expound many things differently from my predecessors—although with their aid, for it was they who first opened the road of inquiry into these things."

Kant expresses his understanding of the difference between mere hypothesis and the proven hypothesis—and thus the status of Copernicus, in his mind—when he summed up his position in the note at Bxxii. The key to the discussion is Kant's overwhelming requirement to achieve certainty: "The change in point of view, analogous to this hypothesis, which is expounded in the *Critique*, I put forward in this preface as an hypothesis only, in order to draw attention to the character of these first attempts at such a change, which are always hypothetical. But in the Critique itself it will be proved, apodeictically not hypothetically. . . . " The revolutionary consequences do not follow from mere hypotheses, but from the hypothesis proven apodeictically. The revolutionary dimensions of Copernicus, and thus Kant, on the analogy he himself draws, will not be ascertained from the study of Copernicus' work alone.

Copernicus tells us in *De Revolutionibus* that not only is the world spherical (I.1),[10] but that "the earth is spherical too" (I.2).[11] For the demonstration of the sphericity of the earth, unlike the "proof" offered by Aristotle in *De Caelo*, that during a lunar eclipse a spherical shadow is cast upon the moon,[12] Copernicus relies on changes in positions of spectators—when people journey northward or southward on the surface of the earth (I.2). Change of position on the surface of the earth brings forth the discovery that the visual contents of the sky change. Moving northward, "many stars situated to the north are not seen to set" and "many to the south are not seen to rise any more."[13] With regard to the earth's movement, Copernicus proceeds along the same lines of reasoning.

> For every apparent change in place occurs on account of the movement either of the thing seen or of the spectator, or on account of the unequal movements of both. For no movement is perceptible relatively to things moved equally in the same directions—I mean relatively to the thing seen and the spectator.[14]

The role of the spectator is explicitly taken up by Copernicus, but this cannot count as sufficient reason to claim that Kant had first hand knowledge of *De Revolutionibus*, nor does any particular astronomical tenet seem particularly relevant to make sense of the general claim of the *Umänderung der Denkart*.

Since the comments of Kant on Copernicus are so brief, it is unclear how Kant understood the doctrines of Copernicus. But, if one reads the commentators on Kant, the contribution of Copernicus is treated either mistakenly or superficially at best. To make sense of Copernicus' hypothesis, and thereby the kind of analogy Kant might have considered, had he considered the matter deeply, we should want to determine what considerations led Copernicus to his conceptual discovery, that is, what conceptual moves did he make, and would these decisions clarify the a priori or a posteriori dimensions of his enterprise? Granted he was dissatisfied with certain tenets of Ptolemaic astronomy. But with what? Shall we follow Birkenmajer and suppose that it was Copernicus' dissatisfaction with

Ptolemy's lunar theory that crucially triggered a change in point of view, hence the heliocentric hypothesis?[15] Or was it, as Swerdlow suggested, Copernicus' study of Regiomantantus' eccentric model of the second anomaly?[16] Dreyer supposed that a fundamental change in point of view was prompted by Copernicus' perception of an annual element in the epicycles of the superior planets and the deferents of Venus and Mercury?[17] Rosen even suggested that it was a reading of the ancients, such as Philolaus and Aristarchus, which first awakened Copernicus from his dogmatic slumbers.[18] Again, shall we follow Ravetz' conjecture that the new model of equinoctial precession, arising in the effort to reform the calendar, brought forth the change in point of view,[19] or shall we follow Wilson's conjecture[20] that the transformation of the annual epicycle into the orbit of the earth, a reinterpretation of the principle of uniform circular motion brought forth Copernicus' *Umänderung der Denkart*. To resolve these questions might be significant, for if no other reason than to better assess what Copernicus believed he was doing, and so—without having to suppose that Kant understands his motivation better than he understood his own—critically assess Kant's account of the origins of the scientific revolution.

In 1959, Norwood Russell Hanson pointed out that Kant had never used the expression "Copernican revolution."[21] Nevertheless, he insisted that there was a significant analogy, which Kant envisaged between his own enterprise and that of Copernicus, the details of which he, alone, of all the commentators supposes Kant to have learned from Wolff. Hanson took the hint from Adickes,[22] who in *Kant als Naturforscher*, in 1924,[23] drew attention to Kant's teaching of mechanics in 1759 and 1760, using Wolff's text; I took the hint from Cassirer, in whose *Kant's Life and Thought*, first published in 1918,[24] he discusses Kant's early teaching career and his use of Wolff's text, and texts of others introduced in 1759. Hanson seems to be the first to recognize Wolff's tutelage of Kant in matters Copernican. He succeeded in making the constructive point that the analogy turns on the transformation "from the conformity of mind to object" to the "conformity of object to mind." For Hanson understands that so long as one supposes that "mind conforms to objects" (*sich nach den Gegenstanden richten*) there is no possibility for Kant to articulate a theory of science, for there is no longer a possibility of a knowledge with certainty. Once we insist that the "mind corresponds to objects," one is committed to a project of seeking to know things-in-themselves, and Kant realized that the pursuit of things-in-themselves could never yield the required certainty, but only empirical generalization.[25] Certainty was possible only if there could be a priori knowledge, only if one could determine beforehand the conditions of knowability. But Hanson never examined the details of that connection with Wolff, although he refers to the relevant text.[26] To show that Hanson's inclination was a sound one—that Kant learned his Copernicus from Wolff—the details of Wolff's exegesis of Copernicus must now be presented.

6.B. The Copernicus That Kant Learned from Wolff

In 1759, Kant wrote to Lindner, "I sit daily at the anvil of my lecturn and keep the heavy hammer of repititious lectures going in some sort of rhythm. Now and then an impulse of a nobler sort, from out of nowhere, tempts me to break out of this cramping sphere, but ever-present need leaps on me with its blustering voice and perpetually drives me back forthwith to hard labor by its threats—*intentat angues atque intonant ore* [he beholds the serpents and his mouth thunders forth]".[27] It was just at this time that Kant began new courses in logic, physical geography, and mechanics. Kant used his own manuscript for the course in physical geography because there was no other text available. Special permission had to be granted because the standard policy was to use only state-approved texts. For the logic, Kant used Meier's text; for the mechanics, Kant used Wolff's *Elementa Mechanicae*, part of a larger work entitled *Elementa Matheseos Universae*. Appended to this work is a study entitled "Commentationem de Studio Matheseos Recte Instituendo"—a treatise on scientific method.[28] Wolff examines the idea of novel hypotheses in order to account for scientific progress; the paradigm example is that of Copernicus, and its subsequent verification by Newton—just the position set forth in the *Critique* at Bxxii, note. The paradigm is astronomy, which Wolff believes has made its advances because of the employment of this method, and he suggests that efforts in both natural philosophy and medicine would have made comparable advances had their enterprises earlier imitated astronomy by implementing this method of novel hypotheses. In 1759 and 1760, as Kant wrote to Lindner, he sat daily at his lecturn and offered repititious lectures from Wolff's dissertation. Perhaps Kant read Copernicus' *De Revolutionibus* firsthand, but it seems all the more likely that the impressions that were most lasting, and with regard to the B Preface of the *Critique* most relevant, can be extracted from Wolff's treatment of Copernicus.

Following the example of Copernicus, Wolff makes several pronouncements in sections 309–12 of the "Commentationem de Studio Matheseos

Recte Instituendo," on the method for scientific progress. (I am not providing a literal translation of the text since it is not necessary for my purposes. I am only concerned to establish a position with selections from Wolff's text exhibit. I provide the context of his remarks whenever surrounding but omitted text requires it. However, I offer the selections from the Latin text in full so that the reader can determine whether the claims I am making seem reasonable.)[29]

(1) In investigating the truths of the sciences—astronomy, physics, and medicine, are specifically under discussion—one must appeal to experience; thus the investigation must proceed a posteriori.

> 310. Ex iis, quae diximus, clarissime perspicitur, quomodo in investigandis veritatibus a posteriori sit procedendum . . .

(2) The use of hypotheses is indispensable to the investigation a posteriori; without their employment, there would be no hope of uncovering the truth.

> 310. . . . quomodo in investigandis veritatibus a posteriori sit procedendum & quam indispensabilis usus sit hypothesium, ut si iisdem uti nolueris, nulla supersit spes veritatis unquam detegendae.

(3) Granting the indispensable character of hypotheses, authors must nevertheless abstain from publishing them until they are definitively proved. This will avoid the problem of circulating mere figments of the imagination, and will thereby avoid the undermining of confidence in the soundness of the scientific enterprise that proceeds profitably only by the use of hypotheses.[30]

> 310. Non est quod excipias hypothesibus equidem locum esse concedendum in inveniendo, ab iis tamen esse abstinendum in libris, qui publici juris fiunt. Etenim ubi veritates ab iis, quae nobis perspecta sunt, principiis procul remotae sunt, ut a priori denegatur ad eas accessus[; cf. also 311:] sed hypotheses ad inveniendum veritatem aptae discernendae a figmentis, quae in eorum locum surrogantur.

(4) Still, employing a method which uses hypotheses is essential. Thus, we should not depreciate the efforts of those who have formulated *false* hypotheses for two reasons: (i) we would probably have made just those errors that others made had not the others made those errors first, and (ii) scientific progress is made by others who take up the earlier efforts which—although alien to the truth (like the theory of concen-

tric spheres)—instruct us as to how we should proceed, when we investigate these hypotheses more deeply.

310. Quamvis igitur examine instituto hypotheses deprehendantur a veritate alienae, non tamen ideo consendae sunt inutiles, propterea quod aberrando a veritate deducimur ad veritatem, ubi methodo conjecturali opus est. Unde memini me saepius auditoribus meis inculcasse, deberi etiam a veritate aberrantibus suas laudes, ubi nobis errandum fuisset, nisi ipsi priores errassent. . . . Nemo Astronomus vitio vertet ei, qui primus de theoria Solis cogitavit, si hypothesin motus aequabilis in orbita concentrica excoluerit, utut successores eam a veritate alienam examine per observationes instituto deprehenderint.

(5) If the physicists had imitated the astronomers by eliciting hypotheses from common observations, and by observations obtained from study and by experiments, correcting and perfecting those things that had been examined, natural philosophy would long ago have made comparable scientific progress to that effected in astronomy.

310. Quodsi Physici Astronomos imitati suissent, ex observationibus communibus eliciendo hypotheses & has per observationes studio quaesitas & experimenta examinatas corrigendo ac perficiendo; nullus profecto dubito, quin Philosophia naturalis dudum magis promota fuisset.

(6) A place for such novel hypotheses must be conceded in Philosophy since it has been made clear that just this method must be employed in the investigation of truth.

311. Discimus etiam, quales esse debeant hypotheses, quibus in Philosophia concendendus est locus; nimirum quas methodus conjecturalis suggerit, qua in veritate investiganda utendum.

(7) But, it remains for us to decide, with regard to scientific method: (i) whether one first ought to observe the phenomena and then inquire into them, or (ii) whether these same things should be deduced a priori from hypotheses, that is, whether one should deduce a priori from hypotheses the things that necessarily follow from them, and then afterward observe whether these same things are in nature.

311. Perinde enim est, sive antea observaris phaenomena & postea demum inquiras, num eadem a priori ex hypothesi deducantur, sive primum a priori deducas ex hypothesi, quae inde necessario consequuntur, & postea demum observes, num eadem quoque in rerum natura ita sese habeant.

(8) The scientific method to be recommended is to start from observations of the phenomena, and then proceed to inquire into them, and to admit nothing into hypotheses except those things gathered from observations; otherwise, we will surely confuse things of which we can be certain with merely imagined things. The supposition of the circular motion of the sun, undermined by Copernicus' hypothesis, is taken as an example: The hypothesis that the sun moves in a circular orbit is "false" or "imaginary" (*commentitius*), but looked at in itself, it is not impossible. This false hypothesis cannot be proved, although even today many still attempt to "force" (*invehunt*) it into natural philosophy, fashioning to serve their own desires, inasmuch as it cannot be demonstrated, they nevertheless imagine to themselves as if such things exist in nature.

311. Quamobrem in Physica . . . maluimus phaenomena ex phaenomenis explicare, nec in hypothesibus admittere nisi quae ex observationibus colliguntur, ne incerta cum certis confundantur & in inventorum numerum referantur, quae sunt in quaestionum numero. Omnium minime autem probamus, si ex commentitiis hypothesibus rationes reddantur in Medicina. . . . Ita sumebatur in Astronomia, orbitam Solis esse circulum. Certum nimirum erat, eam esse lineam in se redeuntem. Quamobrem cum circulus sit linea in se rediens, in se spectatum non impossibile est, ut orbita Solis sit circulus. Non igitur probamus commentitias hypotheses, quas hodie bene multi in Philosophiam naturalem invehunt, quidvis pro lubitu fingentes, utut demonstrare minime possint talia, quae sibi imaginantur, in rerum natura existere posse.

(9) The false hypothesis of the sun's circular orbit is no better than the positing of occult qualities by the scholastics.

311. Immo facile largimur, istiusmodi commenta non esse qualitatibus occultis Scholasticorum meliora.

(10) Therefore, in physics, the preferred method is to proceed from observations to hypotheses, thereby emphasizing the priority of the empirical investigation for forming hypotheses.

311. Quamobrem in Physica . . . maluimus phaenomena ex phaenomenis explicare, nec in hypothesibus admittere nisi quae ex observationibus colliguntur.

(11) Granting the abuse of the hypothetical method—which results in the advancing of false claims—the method must not be abandoned since

it is indispensable for finding truths. But, hypotheses apt for finding truth must be discerned from "figments" that sometimes find their way into the place of suitable hypotheses.

311. Propter abusum tamen hypothesium non tollendus erat usus; sed hypotheses ad inveniendum veritatem aptae discernendae a figmentis, quae in eorum locum surrogantur.

(12) In investigating the truth a posteriori there must be a constant marriage between experience and reason. For even when we assume common observations, in the first place, still nothing is concluded. Following those observations, claims must be deduced a priori from hypotheses that necessarily follow, and without which theories cannot be subjected to examination.

312. . . . in veritate a posteriori investiganda perpetuum esse debere experientiae ac rationis connubium. Neque enim ex observationibus communibus, quae primo loco assumuntur, quicquam concluditur. . . .

(13) Astronomers, like Copernicus, have employed the theory of demonstration—observations (i.e., an appeal to experience) form the basis of hypotheses, which are then examined, the successful results of which are then deduced a priori and shown to follow necessarily. If we want to imitate the astronomers in natural philosophy and in medicine (which is allied to it), we will have to pursue the demonstrative theory.

312. Et ubi ex hypothesi a priori deducenda, quae ex ea necessario consequuntur. . . . Quamobrem si Astronomos in Philosophia naturali, & eidem agnata Medicina imitari velimus; cogitandum erat de theoria demonstrativa.

(14) The directions for a theory of demonstration are supplied by ontology.

312. Ontologia, qualem dedimus, suppeditat notiones directrices. . . .

Wolff was a committed Newtonian. The scientific method he advances is precisely the method of analysis and synthesis, or induction and deduction, promulgated by Newton in both the *Opticks* and *Principia*. Indeed, Kant's specific language more closely resembles Wolff's text than it does Newton's, even if Wolff's treatise is only trying to explicate Newton's expressed doctrine.

In the domain of the empirical sciences, like astronomy and natural philosophy (i.e., physics), the proper method may usefully be called hypothetico-deductive. The specific claims of these sciences cannot be determined a priori but require an investigation a posteriori. This procedure requires that one first makes various kinds of observations or experiments—that is, various appeals to experience—and from this data form hypotheses, by some sort of inductive reasoning. The hypotheses are then examined to determine if they are false/imaginary (*commentitus*) or true. The true hypotheses permit of a rigorous demonstration, a demonstration a priori in which the claim is exhibited to follow necessarily from principles a priori. Wolff's exegesis of the proper scientific method is the same coherence theory of truth adopted by Newton and followed by Kant. It is just this model, articulated in Newton's writings, which Kant had the opportunity to lecture on in the late 1750s and 1760s, a full twenty years before the publication of the first edition of the *Critique*.

This was the method employed by Copernicus, although his novel hypothesis lacked adequate proof. The definitive proof of Copernicus, according to Wolff, rests upon subsequent verification provided by Kepler and Newton. Copernicus thus provides the ingredient—the indispensable method of novel hypotheses—that accounts for the advance in scientific progress that astronomy has made over natural philosophy, and it is methodologically instructive for the progress of science with respect to physics and medicine. Finally, the directions (*notiones directrices*) for this theory of demonstration are supplied, and thus ultimately grounded upon, an ontological or metaphysical theory. With regard to the structure of scientific method, and the strategy of imitating that method to achieve progress in other enterprises, Kant faithfully reproduced Wolff's very words in the *Critique*. Kant's only omission was acknowledging his source.

Kant does not, as does Wolff, distinguish between the specific advance of astronomy over and against natural philosophy. Kant envisages the two to be combined and considered as one whole. Furthermore, mathematics and its hypothetical character are not taken up by Wolff in this study on scientific method, as does Kant (although it is taken up elsewhere in that work). According to the method set out by Wolff, nothing is to enter into hypotheses that does not have some origin in observation/experiment. When Kant mentions Galileo at Bxii, he supposes him to proceed experimentally according to conditions determined beforehand, which he takes to be a priori. Wolff and Kant provide a different emphasis for this activity, but not different positions since Kant surely must suppose that Galileo has reflected long and hard on observations before discovering a priori the conditions of experiment. Even if the emphasis of general a priori constraints on knowledge receives a different weighting in Kant's exposition, the overall effect provides just the sort of clue that this study sought in appraising Copernicus' influence upon Kant: the Kantian source of his thinking about Copernicus. Importantly, the special and innovative contribution by Copernicus is highlighted here by Wolff; indeed, Wolff makes many references to Copernicus in his writings, as could surely be expected from an author who writes the definitive Prussian text on mechanics and astronomy.

In 1759 and 1760, at the anvil of his lectern, Kant wearily and repititiously presented just this text of Wolff. A close inspection of that text supplies just the sort of fundamental ingredients that Kant introduces in the B Preface to the *Critique of Pure Reason*. Granted that the references to Copernicus are so meager, one can only hazard a guess about sources of influence. Still, the view of Copernicus presented in the *Critique* is in very close accord with that propounded by Wolff, and lectured by Kant. With this information before us, is it more likely to suppose that Kant, citing Copernicus, is thinking about *De Revolutionibus*, or rather Wolff's summary and critical comment on the introduction of novel hypotheses—identified with Copernicus and subsequently verified by Kepler and Newton—when he writes the B Preface? Kant surely might have read Copernicus' *De Revolutionibus* firsthand, as Kemp Smith supposed; I doubt it. But more importantly, it seems far more likely that Kant had in mind—even if unconsciously—Wolff's "Commentationem de Studio Matheseos Recte Instituendo," appended to the *Elementa Mechanicae*, which he lectured for at least two years, than any passage from the work of Copernicus, when he wrote the B Preface.[31]

Rethinking the Revolutionary Contributions of Copernicus and Galileo to the Natural Science That Kant Understood

7.A. The Revolutionary Consequences of Copernicus' Hypothesis: Toward a Transformation in the Traditional Disciplinary Matrix

Der Narr will die ganze Kunst Astronomiae umkehren.—Martin Luther on Copernicus, 1539

IN HIS RECENT WORK, *REVOLUTIONS IN SCIENCE*, I. BERNARD COHEN ANSWERS the question "Was there a Copernican Revolution?" by declaring "If there was a revolution in astronomy, that revolution was Keplerian or Newtonian, and not in any simple or valid sense Copernican."[1] On the contrary, Kuhn's view, in *The Copernican Revolution* (1957), which has become a commonplace, is expressed in his opening sentence: "The Copernican Revolution was a revolution in ideas, a transformation in man's conception of the universe and of his own relation to it. . . . A reform in the fundamental concepts of astronomy is therefore the first of the Copernican Revolution's meanings."[2] The problems inherent in thinking about Kant's alleged Copernican revolution are to be found when reappraising the historical context of Copernicus' own achievement.

The results of such a reappraisal suggest that the radical and sudden transformation that the word "revolution" suggests, and which is why it is usefully employed, is misapplied to Copernicus, whose achievements are more modest and less radical than the word implies. At the same time, the review intimates perhaps a revolutionary consequence, not in astronomy proper, but in terms of a radical revision of the hierarchical classification of the liberal arts—the ingenious suggestion by Robert Westman. The transformation in that disciplinary matrix opened the way to a new theory of demonstration, and thus the acceptance of the scientific method that determined what could count as a proof. A clearer understanding of this new possibility of demonstration is illuminating for an understanding of the apodeictic certainty that Kant believed he secured in the *Critique*. Before we examine Kant's transcendental deduction, a brief reassessment of Copernicus' achievement is in order. The desired result is to understand more deeply how we have been led astray about and by Kant, with regard to Copernicus.

Suppose we wonder whether the earth is: (a) at rest, as it appears to common sense, relative to the apparent motion of the sun and fixed stars, or (b) in motion, contrary to our commonsense experience, and is in fact a planet, a body both rotating and revolving relative to the sun and the fixed stars. How shall we decide one way or the other? What should count as proof, that is, what could count as a demonstration? Perhaps we should say, from our present point of view, that an adequate proof or demonstration was the sort provided by Bessel, who not merely detected but measured stellar parallax, or even Foucault who experimentally demonstrated the earth's rotation by the use of his pendulum. In any event, Kant is satisfied that Newton's formulation of the laws of motion, which also "yielded proof" (Bxxii, note) of the universal gravitation "which holds the universe together," provided the needed demonstration, and so "gave established certainty" to Copernicus' novel hypothesis that the earth, indeed, is in motion. What does this suggest to us about how Kant understood demonstration?

If Kant did not know the contents of Galileo's *Dialogues Concerning Two Chief World Systems* (1632), it could only be because he never took the book off of his own library shelf.[3] According to the catalogue of Kant's books auctioned in 1808, which Arthur Warda discovered and published in 1922, Kant owned a 1699 edition of Galileo's *Systema cosmicum*. In addition, Kant taught the *Elementa Mechanicae* in 1759 and 1760, and in that work Wolff refers to Galileo. In the larger *Elementa Matheseos Universae*, there are other references to Galileo, including mention of *In Dialogis de Systemate mundi* by name.[4]

In the *Dialogue*, which Galileo first thought to entitle *On the Ebb and Flow of the Tides*, the final section called the "Fourth Day," permits Galileo to present his proof or demonstration of the Copernican hypothesis. The proof Galileo offers is the phenomenon of tides, the motion of which he claims cannot be accounted for unless we suppose that the earth is in motion. The combination of two motions, the daily rotation and the yearly revolution, Galileo believed were necessary and sufficient to explain that phenomenon: "It has already been decided that the monthly and annual periodic alterations of the tides could be derived from no other cause than from the varying ratios between the annual motion [of the earth] and the additions to it and subtractions from it of the diurnal rotation."[5]

The argument is unfortunate for several reasons, not least of which was that the tides were known from antiquity to have a triple period, and the basic period of ebb and flow is slightly more than twelve hours, resulting usually in approximately two tides every day. The problem of accounting for ebb and flow and the monthly variation of tides had been supposed to be connected with the moon long before Galileo. Galileo dismisses the influence of the moon as "vain fantasy."[6] It would be fair to say that the argument of the "Fourth Day" won over few converts. Either Kant does not know of the purported proof, or he dismisses it. In any case, he does not mention it. It is thus not included as a demonstration of Copernicus' novel hypothesis.

Newton's proof of the laws of motion, in Kant's estimation, does provide the required demonstration. He does not detail the argument but we can make a reasonable reconstruction from Wolff's text, both in the "De Studio Astronomiae," chapter 9 of the fifth volume of the *Elementa Matheseos Universae*, under the general heading "Commentationem de Praecipuis Scriptis Mathematicis,"[7] and in the following and final section of that large work, the "Commentationem de Studio Mathematico Recte Instituendo." In both places the argument traces a development from Copernicus to Kepler to Newton. In the "De Studio Astronomiae," the hypotheses of ancient and more recent astronomers are spoken of. Among the more recent, Copernicus provides the "true system of the world," Kepler presents the "true orbits of the planets and their laws of motion," and Newton finally uncovers and definitively demonstrates "at last, the physical causes of all things"—the general laws of motion and universal gravitation (sections 22 and 16). That same text is provided in the German version of Wolff's *Elementa Matheseos Universae*, which was entitled *Die Anfangs-Gründe aller mathematischen Wissenschaften*. The German version was first published in 1710, the Latin version, intended to reach the wider audience, was published 1713–15. Kant owned the first edition of the Latin text, and the 1750 edition of the German. Both texts are roughly parallel (section 22 in the Latin version mirrors section 222 in the German):

22. . . . *Copernici, Kepleri,* atque *Newtoni* inventis superstructam, quorum ille verum systema mundi, iste veras planetarum orbitas ac motuum leges, hic tandem omnium causas physicas detexit.[8]

16. Hanc theoriam [having just referred to universal gravitation] causas physicis convenientem demonstravit *Newtonus* lib. 3 *Princ. Mathem. Philos. Nat.*[9]

222. . . . nachdem *Copernicus* das wahre systema mundi auf die Bahn gebracht, *Kepler* die richtigen Gesetze der Bewegung entdectet, und Newton ihre Ursachen ausgemacht.[10]

In the "Commentationem de Studio Mathematico Recte Instituendo," section 309 of "De Studio Astronomiae" begins with the hypotheses of Copernicus and Kepler:

Theoricam tradidimus juxta hypothesin *Copernici* atque *Kepleri*, nimirum supposito Terrae motu & orbitis planetarum ellipticis, in quibus Planetae ea lege incedunt.[11]

Although Newton is viewed as the one who demonstrated the physical causes of the motions hypothesized, Wolff points out that his success did not arise from "eliminating hypotheses" but rather by making use of them himself, even if it be supposed that the comment from the General Scholium—"I feign no hypotheses"—declares them contraband. "Laudant quidam Newtonum, quod ex Philosophia naturali eliminaverit hypotheses, qui tamen hypothesibus indulget in iis ipsis, in quibus eum ab iisdem abstinuisse existimant."[12]

The Copernican hypothesis—the claim for the earth's mobility—finds subsequent verification in Kepler's hypothesis of the elliptical motion of the planets, and Newton's demonstration of the physical causes of all things, in the general laws of motion and universal gravitation. Kant following Wolff, seems to have supposed that Newton's demonstration consisted in showing that elliptical planetary paths imply an inverse-square law for the force operating on bodies moving in just those paths. Since the supposition of elliptical planetary orbits was worked out by Kepler from the exacting observations of Tycho Brahe concerning the planet Mars, which make no uniform sense for an orbit around the earth, Wolff-Kant would have had some good reason to suppose that Newton's *Principa* provided a demonstration of Copernicus' heliocentric hypothesis. Thus, the proof for the mobility of the earth—from Kant's point of view—required that Copernicus' hypothesis led to Kepler's discovery and deduction of elliptical planetary orbits, only on the supposition of Copernicus' heliocentric hypothesis; and then had Newton systematically show that the planets—the earth among them—were required to move in just the path Kepler predicted around the sun as a result of a universal gravitation that exercised a force on a body that varied inversely in proportion to the square of the distance between the planetary body and the sun.[13] Thus, the orbits that the planets occupy, the planets had to occupy necessarily; they could not be anywhere else on the presumption that an inverse square force was operating on them. For Kant, Newton's demonstration was mathematical, precisely the kind of proof that Kant and his contemporaries could accept as a demonstration. But, when Copernicus offered his hypothesis ensconced in the detailed mathematical theory, it could not have been accepted as a demonstration. To Copernicus' dilemma—how does one demonstrate the motion of the earth—a supposition contrary to common sense, we now turn.

"If anything can be called revolutionary in Copernicus' work," writes Robert S. Westman, it is that " . . . Copernicus argued for the earth's status as a planet by appealing to arguments from the mathematical part of astronomy. In so doing he shifted the weight of evidence for the earth's planetary status to the lower discipline of geometry, thereby violating the traditional hierarchy of the disciplines."[14] Westman recognized that the status of the heliocentric hypothesis rested on a new kind of appeal and thereby required a review of what could count for the demonstration of an hypothesis.

According to the dominant medieval classification scheme, inspired by Aristotelian influence, the hierarchical system of disciplines treats mathematics on a lower level than natural philosophy or physics. The higher order science deals with causes as a way to express the being or essence of a thing, while mathematics is a secondary science of quantity. According to Aristotle's texts, natural philosophy (physics) deals with essence, what a thing is, while mathematics merely tells us how much. The significance of making this distinction, ordering the disciplines hierarchically, is to provide guidance when there may be a conflict in views. On the Aristotelian model, a conflict between mathematical and physical claims is easily resolved. The guidance comes from the higher discipline, namely physics, whose concern is causes and thereby the essential nature of things, and not merely a quantitative determination of those same things. The texts of Aristotle advise one to take the advice of physics over mathematics, should a conflict arise between them.[15] The dominant medieval classification scheme, inspired by one reading of Aristotle, characterized the hierarchical organization of the liberal arts in just this fashion in the time of Copernicus.

This distinction between mathematics as opposed to physics became all the more significant following the work of Ptolemy,[16] who certainly envisages his contribution as following in just this tradition. Ptolemy proposed an alternative astronomy to the theory of concentric spheres, first proposed by Eudoxus and embraced by Aristotle. That theory failed to explain why the planets vary in brightness. It also could not account for their movement northerly-southerly on the required supposition that each heavenly body made a single and simple motion.[17] Ptolemy's alternative account—still embracing Aristotle's demand that celestial motion is uniform, circular, and simple—proposed two mathematical devices—the epicycle and deferent—to account for variations in planetary speed and brightness.[18] We were now to suppose that the planet moves uniformly about a small circle (i.e., epicycle), while the center of that small circle moved uniformly about a larger circle (i.e., deferent). Ptolemy's introduction of yet another mathematical invention, the equant, produced from the point of view of prediction a successful model. But the equant also created a problem outside of its mathematical usefulness for prediction. For the physical reality that the Ptolemaic model projects is not so easy to embrace, as its predictive utility. As Westman put it "Here the center of an epicycle revolves nonuniformly as viewed both from the sphere's center and from the earth but uniformly as computed from a point that sits a distance from the earth's center equal to twice that of earth. . . . But now ask how it can be that the planet, like a bird or fish, 'knows' how to navigate uniformly in a circle about an off-center point while, simultaneously, flying variably with respect to the center of the same sphere."[19] In response to this sort of objection, astronomers at the universities in Copernicus' time treated "planetary circles" separately from the "spheres" in which they were embedded. The conflict between the mathematical and physical parts of astronomy were thus avoided by keeping the questions separate.[20] Whenever there was a conflict—following the restatement of the Aristotelian hierarchy by and as interpreted by Albertus Magnus[21] —the mathematical sciences were conceived as inferior to physics. But Copernicus sought to reconcile the conflict he encountered between the mathematical and physical parts of astronomy. The heliocentric hypothesis, the argument for the earth's status as a planet—a physical claim— Copernicus sought to demonstrate by an appeal to the mathematical part of astronomy.

From this perspective, the success of Copernicus' hypothesis would signal a revolutionary revision of the disciplinary matrix, a reordering of the hierarchy of the liberal arts. Not merely a review of the order of things, Copernicus' method effectively challenged the foundation of a dominant classification scheme, and hence challenged the very meaning of what could count as a demonstration.

Copernicus' *De Revolutionibus*, however, was not received this way. The Church, with other pressing problems, found itself surprisingly little troubled. But this was because it chose to read it as a mere hypothesis, a mathematical device that ultimately could make no claim to physical reality. The initial reaction from the Church effectively testifies that the very kind of demonstration that Kant can accept, from the mathematical part of astronomy, had undergone a revolutionary reordering in the ensuing three-hundred-odd years, and apparently he did not appreciate this transformation, for he believes that mathematics had entered onto the "sure path of a science" already in Greek antiquity.

The publication of Copernicus' *De Revolutionibus*, entrusted to the impassioned disciple Rheticus, turned the matter over to Andreas Osiander, who took it upon himself to add an unsigned prefatory letter to the front of the manuscript. That this appended letter was not the work of Copernicus' was known already in the sixteenth century before Kepler. Kepler (1609), and then Gassendi in his *Life of Copernicus* (1654),[22] revealed Osiander's authorship. But as Hanson pointed out, many readers believed it was the work of Copernicus; even Kemp Smith did not recognize this and thereby misunderstands the meaning of "hypotheses" for Copernicus in terms of guidance provided there.[23]

One important result of taking Osiander's appended letter as if it were by Copernicus, is to misunderstand how Copernicus understood the import of his own work. If one passes over that letter and seeks Copernicus' vision in the *De Revolutionibus* proper, the claim becomes much stronger, with far more definite commitment to a physical interpretation. The physical realism of the claims in *De Revolutionibus* stand in marked contrast to the hypothetical character insisted upon in the prefatory letter. It seems that Osiander had become convinced that various groups would object to Copernicus' work because they would realize that otherwise "the liberal arts, established long ago on a correct basis, would be thrown into confusion." Osiander's letter, by insisting upon the status of the work as a "mere hypothesis," constituted a renunciation of "physical truth" or even probability. The letter portrays the work as a strictly mathematical-astronomical text. It thereby removed itself from possible conflict with physics, that is natural philosophy, and thus the physical part of astronomy whose study was kept separate from the mathematical in the universities.

Despite the strength of the physical claims made in the text of *De Revolutionibus*, Wolff and Kant regarded Copernicus' work as constituting a mere hypothesis, not a deduction. In a word, Copernicus was not thought by them to have given a demonstration for his hypothesis of terrestrial mobility. Even if Wolff knew that Osiander, and not Copernicus himself, was the author of the prefatory letter—and that seems likely since it seems that Wolff knew firsthand Kepler's 1609 *Astronomia Nova*, which reveals that fact—nevertheless, Wolff and Kant seem to accept the prefatory remarks as indicative of the status of Copernicus' achievement. This helps to clarify why Wolff places such an emphasis upon Copernicus' introduction of novel hypotheses that yet require a rigorous demonstration, because in itself, the hypothesis yields no demonstration of its physical reality. According to the closing sentence of Osiander's letter the whole enterprise amounted to this: "And as far as hypotheses go, let no one expect anything in the way of certainty from astronomy, since astronomy can offer us nothing certain, lest, if anyone take as true that which has been constructed for another use, he go away from this discipline a bigger fool than when he came to it."[24]

Kant regarded Copernicus' achievement in accordance with the sentiment expressed in that appended letter, even though the body of *De Revolutionibus* surely sought to make claims far more definitive than restrictions suggested in the apologia of that letter. For Kant, following Wolff, Copernicus advances a novel hypothesis about the motion of the earth, whose definitive demonstration consisted in Newton's full-blown theory, integrating terrestrial and celestial motions, having already adopted the Copernican hypothesis as a point of departure. Seen in this way, Newton's demonstration contains within it the hypothesis of Copernicus. Kant envisaged his own work on the order of Newton's demonstration. In this case, Kant's novel hypothesis—the transformation of point of view whereby objects must conform to mind—Kant says in the 'B' Preface is introduced hypothetically but will be proved apodeictically—which means a rigorous deduction—in the *Critique* itself. So, as the Copernican hypothesis is to Newton's *Principia* so the Kantian hypothesis (of the B Preface) is to the *Critique of Pure Reason*: Kant's Newtonian Revolution in Philosophy.

Thus, the very idea of a demonstration undergoes serious transition from 1543 through 1781, and that transition announces a reorganization of a traditional disciplinary matrix, a reassessment of the dominant medieval classification of the hierarchy of the liberal arts, whereby the authority of the Church—whose special claim to that authority is rendered by the Aristotelian-inspired program of placing theology among the highest disciplines—had to renew its vision both of itself and the world by permitting instruction and correction from the science of quantity—mathematics. With the increasing emphasis on empirical confirmation, other changes would be required for a theory of demonstration, including a new plan about the logic of demonstration. Kant inherits and transforms this tradition, and so to it we now turn briefly.

7.B. Aristotle, Galileo, and Kant:
Toward a Transformation in the Logic of Demonstration

When Kant advances his transcendental deduction, he believes his argument to provide apodeictic proof. The argument structure of that deduction is a species of the hypothetico-deductive method, or analysis-synthesis, or induction-deduction. This argument structure is incompatible with the expressed declarations of Aristotle in the *Posterior Analytics*, and the dominant medieval classification scheme, inspired by Aristotelianism, which mollified the impact of Copernicus' argument for the mobility of the earth. The way to Kant's demonstrative strategy was paved by Galileo. Recent work in the history of science requires that we rethink the sources that motivated Newton, and Wolff, and thus subsequently, Kant's project. This naturally leads to a brief reassessment of Galileo's purported revolutionary contribution to scientific method.

The thesis to be argued is twofold: (i) Galileo was not anti-Aristotelian; he adamantly challenged the Aristotelianism in the Italian universities but embraced the Aristotelianism as taught at the Collegio Romano—this requires that we rethink Aristotle's text in light of conflicting schools that all proclaimed Aristotelian inspiration, and (ii) Galileo, while accepting the fundamental Aristotelian program that searches for causes and essences, transforms Aristotle's model of demonstration to make permissible, not only the deduction of a conclusion from premises, but the necessary inference of premises from conclusions. This attempt to justify the inference of premises from causes, Aristotle dismisses as unjustifiable induction; and yet, if an empirical or a posteriori science is to be secured, causes (equals premises) must be capable of being inferred from observations (equals conclusions). If Galileo's efforts yielded revolutionary consequences, it seems most sound to identify that contribution in terms of the transformation he effects in the logic of demonstration: the formulation of the demonstrative regress argument.

The problem of demonstration is discussed by Aristotle at length in the *Organon*, most especially in the *Posterior Analytics*.[25] A central matter confronting an interpretation of Aristotle's enterprise is somehow to reconcile two tendencies in his work. On the one hand, the theory of the syllogism (*sullogismos*) in the *Prior Analytics*, and the demonstrative syllogism (*apodeixis*) in the *Posterior Analytics*, provide a rigorous theory of scientific methodology. But, on the other hand, an inspection of scientific works—physical or biological—like *De Caelo*, *Generation of Animals*, et alia, provides little sign of implementing the practice that that highly formalized theory required. The tension brought forth by

Aristotle's treatment of the demonstrative syllogism is that the theory seems to demand a rigorous formal approach, while Aristotle's actual practice rarely, if ever, makes use of just that formality. Indeed, it has been rightly suggested that even in the *Posterior Analytics* there is not a single perfect example of a demonstration.

In 1949, Sir David Ross insisted that the *Posterior Analytics* is a study of scientific method.[26] But, in 1969, Jonathan Barnes, dissatisfied with this view on the grounds that Aristotle does not seem to employ that method when he details his scientific researches, reached a different conclusion: "In developing a theory of demonstration and in constructing his notion of a demonstrative science, Aristotle was not telling the scientist how to construct his research; he was giving pedagogical advice on the most efficient and economic method for bettering his charges. The theory of demonstration offers a formal account of how an achieved body of knowledge should be presented and thought."[27] In 1981, Guthrie responded to Barnes, taking Ross' position, by arguing that such a pedagogical method is incompatible with the explicit claims in the *Topics* where Aristotle subscribes to dialectic as the primary pedagogical method for imparting scientific knowledge.[28] But Guthrie offered no good argument to account for the lack of implementation of the method when Aristotle conducts his scientific researches.

Controversies surrounding Aristotelian-inspired scientific research and demonstration were no more settled in Copernicus' time. Different schools, proclaiming to be following Aristotle's instruction, proposed varying and conflicting positions about the purpose in and method of the *Posterior Analytics*. The problem of demonstration for Copernicus emerged when his mathematical proof faced a tradition, which in believing itself to embrace Aristotle's project, could not accept a mathematical proof as a challenge to physical claims already established by the Church under the guidance of the higher discipline of theology. Those to whom the work of Copernicus was directed were not compelled to take seriously the challenge to previously accepted physical claims—in the manner that Copernicus, no doubt, intended—because the dominant classification scheme of the hierarchy of the liberal arts could not accommodate Copernicus' mathematical formulations as a successful refutation of those physical claims. Galileo encountered a similar problem in the very formal mechanism of the logic of demonstration itself.

The demonstrative syllogism discussed in the *Posterior Analytics* depends upon principles. Those principles must be true, necessary and universal, immediate, and explanatory of the conclusion. All demonstrations presuppose principles that are themselves indemonstrable, and the argument proceeds from premises that are "more knowable in themselves" to conclusions that are "more familiar to us." The procedure, demonstratively, was thereby one-directional, from premises to conclusions, from the clarity of a knowledge more universal to a demonstration of a statement whose necessary connection and hence universal status was validly assured through an inheritance from the argument's structure.

Debates over Aristotle's scientific method arose because the employment of empirical methods requires, not only the demonstration of a conclusion from premises, but also the inference of premises from a conclusion—a conclusion which might itself be an observation. The empirical dimension of the enterprise required the validation of a procedure that seems to be ruled out of hand by the mechanism of Aristotelian demonstration itself, since it would require a justification of induction—not a one-directional mode of inference but a two-directional mode. The attempt to infer the premises from the conclusion is not demonstratively sanctioned in Aristotle's *Posterior Analytics*.

The distinction Aristotle draws in the *Posterior Analytics* between the *hoti* argument—a knowledge of the fact that later Aristotelians tended to call a demonstration *quia*—and the truly demonstrative *dioti* argument—a knowledge of the reasoned fact that later Aristotelians tended to call a demonstration *propter quid*—amounted to a matter of determining which argument, indeed, supplied the cause of a thing, and thereby its essence.[29] The *dioti* argument, or *propter quid*, provided the required demonstration of the reasoned fact, because it supplied the reason or cause. The problem was to justify the employment of a new mode of demonstration that integrated the *quia* and *propter quid* arguments. William Wallace in his impressive study, *Galileo and His Sources*, has shown that the resolution Galileo offered he called the "demonstrative regress." I turn to Galileo now since the demonstrative regress argument that he systematically employs outlines just that hypothetico-deductive model set out by Wolff, for which Copernicus' novel hypothesis is a paradigm. Again, it is this model, new to the fifteenth and sixteenth centuries, that Kant embraces and calls upon as a model for his work in metaphysics.

In his treatment of *Logical Questions*,[30] Galileo is, in this sense, preoccupied with the question of whether or not there is a demonstrative regress, a valid form of demonstrative argument that permits inference both from premises to conclusions and from conclusions back to premises. As Wallace put in his recent work, *Galileo and his Sources*:

The problem of the regress arises from the proposal of ancient philosophers who wished the demonstrative process to exhibit perfect circularity, in the sense that the conclusion would be known perfectly through the premises, and the premises through the conclusion. The proposal was rejected by Aristotle, who offered in its stead an imperfect type of circle wherein premises could sometimes be inferred from a conclusion by a demonstration *quia*, and then the same conclusion deduced from the premises by a demonstration *propter quid*—a twofold *progressus* or two *progressiones* that came to be known as a demonstrative *regressus*.[31]

Wallace claims that Galileo made use of, and in this sense perfected, the demonstrative regress. The effect would have been perceived to undermine the Aristotelian project engaged in at the Italian universities. But, Wallace's intriguing case is that Galileo supposed himself to be perpetuating, not undermining, an Aristotelian program. The commonplace has been, as Burtt[32] and many others have long suggested, that Galileo proceeds contrary to Aristotle. Wallace has shown that Galileo subscribes to programs following the Aristotelians—not in the Italian universities—but those at the Collegio Romano. The case he has made is that although Galileo makes use of a demonstrative argument form, not explicitly formulated in Aristotle, he does so as if he is still pursuing an essentially Aristotelian program: a search for causes and essences.

Criticizing the Aristotelians of his day, Galileo's diatribe was directed more or less to the Aristotelians at the Italian universities, but not to Aristotelians per se, or their reformulated program. So Wallace can say, "The Aristotelian ideal of scientific knowledge is that of *cognitio certa per causes*, that is, knowledge that is certain through causes, or knowledge that cannot be otherwise because it is based on the causes that make a thing be the way they are. . . . Now Galileo . . . never once did he depart from this ideal of certain and irreversible knowledge, as the goal of his investigations . . . never once did he question the ideal. . . . "[33]

The constructive position put forth by Wallace amounts to this: "It should be quite clear that there was nothing novel in the ideal of science to which Galileo subscribed.[34] Galileo, rather than being the revolutionary who overthrew the Aristotelian program, apparently embraced it at its foundation. By advancing his claims through the demonstrative regress argument, Galileo advanced a novel hypothesis that sought to make the logic of demonstration serviceable to the recognized and indispensable element of experience, with its empirical foundation. Galileo thus envisages a program bequeathed by Aristotle, and in a manner like

Copernicus who sought to return to the earlier, pristine vision of the ancients. In Wallace's provocative study, the revolutionary contribution of Galileo is reassessed.

In this process of trying to recover an ancient wisdom, Copernicus brought about a social revolution—if we may speak this way—in the hierarchy of the disciplinary matrices, in the hierarchical order of the dominant medieval classification scheme; Galileo contributed to a revolution in the logic of demonstration by making use of the demonstrative regress. When Wolff insists that no hypotheses can be properly formed without observation/experiment, and thereafter a rigorous demonstration a priori must be provided,[35] he is echoing the methodological disposition of Galileo's enterprise. Whether Wolff envisions Galileo as his source is yet another matter. More important is the novel hypothesis articulated in transforming the ideal of a logic of demonstration. If rigorous demonstration a priori could be supplied, then the necessary inference from the conclusion back to the premises can be defended since the supposed connection is necessary. Both the ideological moves contributed by Copernicus and Galileo inform Kant's project in the *Critique of Pure Reason*.

In the *Critique*, Kant can treat mathematics on a par with natural science. One way he expresses this connection is by insisting upon the synthetic character of mathematical propositions.[36] He can thereby accept Newton's *Principia* as a demonstrative proof that gave established certainty to Copernicus' novel hypothesis, and can accept the novel hypothesis as that indispensable ingredient without which Newton's discovery would have been impossible. He can make use of lessons attempted by Galileo, in the logic of demonstration, whether he learned these maneuvers from Galileo or not, since he surely learned this same methodological constraint from Wolff, when he formulates the foundation of his own demonstration in the "Transcendental Deduction" and the "Refutation of Idealism." Even though Kant regards himself to be making no contributions to logic, which in his estimation had entered onto the secure path of a science long ago,[37] and has not been required since Aristotle to retrace even a single step, the transcendental argument that Kant relies upon to provide his rigorous deduction bears little resemblance to anything in Aristotle. Nor does even his own table of judgments, doubtlessly gotten from Meier's text which he taught in 1759 and following,[38] and other Aristotelian treatises on logic like it, reproduce anything that can be found in Aristotle. More like Galileo's enterprising utilization of the demonstrative regressus, which treated the empirical elements in experience as crucial and capable of providing rigorous deduction, Kant will try to connect the a priori and empirical/intuitional dimensions of experience by formulating and utilizing a new logical device for demonstration. Whether or not we can call this formulation by Kant revolutionary is yet another matter.

I turn now in chapter 8, to examine the synthetic a priori project to exhibit, on the order of Copernicus' novel hypothesis, the hypothetical moment on which Kant models his demonstration, and then turn in chapter 9 to consider the rigorous deduction that gives expression to Kant's logic of demonstration. Are either of these aspects of Kantian demonstration sufficient to justify his claim that he has effected a revolution in philosophy? I think the answer is yes; but curiously enough, not for the reasons he supposed.

Kant's Copernican Hypothesis: Science, Metaphysics, and the Pursuit of Synthetic a priori Judgments

8.A. Kant's Novel Hypothesis

ACCORDING TO THE WOLFF-KANT PROGRAM, THE NATURAL SCIENCES, LIKE astronomy and physics, developed rapidly and found their way to a secure path of science, by way of the utilization of novel hypotheses—a conjectural method that supplied programmatic or regulative guidance in discovering the course of nature. That scientific method Kant adapts for his science of metaphysics. The result was a transformation in the idea of a demonstration—what counts as a proof for a claim. Kant's theory of demonstration can be examined in two respects: (1) the novel hypothesis—on analogy with Copernicus—the pursuit of synthetic a priori judgments as the fundamental principles that ground any knowledge claim whatsoever, that the fundamental ground of our knowledge is not logical but epistemological; and (2) a rigorous deduction—on analogy with Newton's model of analysis and synthesis—which consists in (a) the metaphysical deduction that exhibits the result of analysis or induction, and (b) the transcendental deduction that, in revealing the immediately certain principles which are not obvious and so must be demonstrated, follows Newton's model of synthesis. The deductions constitute Kant's specific reply to the sceptical challenge of the impossibility of knowing that there are external objects, and that there is some enduring self to which one and all of my experiences may be referred.

The purportedly revolutionary pursuit of synthetic a priori judgments is taken up here in section 8.B. The theory of the rigorous deduction will be taken up next in chapter 9. In both cases, the following metaphor is operative: Kant's method constitutes a *Versuch*, a trial. The investigation of the faculty of the understanding is an examination of the legislative faculty, the faculty which judges, which prescribes to nature its laws.[1] The use of an *Experimentalmethode* or *Versuch* is intended to provide a test for the hypothesis that he seeks to prove apodeictically. In both cases, what a judge and the experimental method have in common—and this is why Kant exploits the metaphor—is that both are concerned with trials. Hence, Kant's novel hypothesis is a *Versuch* in both senses. In the twofold deduction, Kant will explicate his trial by an appeal to the metaphors of Roman jurisprudence, introducing first an investigation *quid facti* and then one *quid juris*. Reason, like an appointed judge, will compel nature to answer its questions. This procedure expresses Kant's novel hypothesis, and the revolutionary character of the epistemological turn he claims to advance.

8.B. Was Kant's Novel Hypothesis about the Foundation of Certain Knowledge Revolutionary?

Kant's novel hypothesis about the foundation of certain knowledge is his supposition that the principles of knowledge are synthetic a priori. In this section, the meaning of this hypothesis and its historical context will be explored. The result of that investigation will show that although the manner in which Kant proposes his hypothesis is systematically new, it is not as novel as he would lead us to believe. Thus, to suppose it to be revolutionary was an overstatement on his part, although the consequences that ultimately followed for the discipline perhaps deserve to be called revolution-making. This position can only be defended if we shall grant that the *Critique of Pure Reason* deserves to be viewed as radically changing the historical program of philosophy, shifting its agenda away from a search for things-in-themselves, and declaring such a program to be hopeless.

The character of a science is revealed, for Kant, through the synthetic a priori judgments that constitute its foundation. The structure of science, like every object of theoretical knowledge for Kant, is determined by the structure that we impose upon and in our experience. The structure of science turns out to be the structure of objective knowledge, whose foundation finds expression in synthetic a priori judgments. For the question of how the world is is discovered to mean—*mit den ersten Gedanken des Kopernicus*—how must the world be—so far as I impose conditions upon experience—in order to be an object for me. The traditional metaphysics, which supposed that objects have a real nature and the mind comes to grasp that real nature if and when it conforms to the nature of the object, is transformed by the critical or transcendental turn in philosophy to determine the conditions to which the object must conform in order to be a possible object of experience for me. This critical turn finds expression in the emphasis upon synthetic a priori judgments.

Kant's pursuit of the possibility of a metaphysics proves to be the pursuit of the nature of science, an attempt to show how mathematics and natural science can be sciences, that is, how synthetic a priori judgments are possible in them, at their foundation, which in turn grounds the other judgments upon them. And having shown how they are possible, Kant turns to metaphysics, to demonstrate how synthetic a priori judgments are possible, and thus how it is that metaphysics can be put on "the secure path of a science"—on *der sichere Gang einer Wissenschaft*—as are mathematics and natural science, because metaphysics would thus be shown to be a science too. The character of that science can be uncovered by delving more deeply into the meaning of the synthetic a priori judgment. When that character becomes clear, we shall then be in a position to discover how the goal of science is certainty, and that certainty takes on a special meaning, namely, to determine beforehand or in advance (*vorbereitet*) of any particular experience the limiting constraints on how the world can be discovered by us.

It is important to emphasize the special relation between Kant's attempt to render a meaningful metaphysics on the one hand, and definitively answer the question "What is science?" on the other, in the first *Critique*. The propositions of science ultimately rest upon a system of principles even more general than the laws of motion set out in Newton's *Principia*.[2] Although these principles prove to be metaphysical they are shared by the other sciences and are supposed to underlie their respective validity. Interestingly enough, for Kant the metaphysical principles are the fruitful consequence of the attempt to demonstrate how synthetic a priori judgments are possible in natural science. In this sense, the fundamental propositions that natural science must suppose for its very possibility are metaphysical. To say this is to characterize what natural science ostensibly is: an enterprise the fundamental constraints of which are imposed a priori, that is beforehand (*vorbereitet*), even if the specific determinations must be discovered a posteriori. In Kant's estimation this is the only reliable way to achieve certainty in that enterprise.

Science, for Kant, just as Wallace has shown for Galileo, still retains the Aristotelian character of the search for certainty even if it is not of causes per se. If the principles of metaphysics characterize the foundation of every system of thought deserving to be called a science, then it would be true to say that natural science has a more privileged status than does mathematics to that fundamental structure. For all the judgments of mathematics are synthetic a priori, and yet not a single one of them Kant supposes is metaphysical. On the other hand, every one of the twelve (eight?) synthetic a priori judgments,[3] which articulate the conditions of understanding—which we bring to and impose upon experience—and the foundations of natural science—one and all—coincide with the metaphysical.[4] The pursuit of natural science and metaphysics, then, is a search for the same foundation. That natural science shares its foundation with the articulated principles of metaphysics—but only derivatively, suggests that natural science was a secondary enterprise within the Kantian disciplinary matrix insofar as it could not by itself reveal its own foundations, its own presuppositions.

The position that synthetic a priori judgments constitute the foundation of any system deserving to be called a science represents what Kant claims is a new strategy in philosophy. This purportedly new strategy is what I am calling Kant's novel hypothesis on the Copernican analogy. Did Kant have good reason to suppose that this novel hypothesis was either original or revolutionary? The answer I believe is no, but not simply. In order to clarify the status of his novel hypothesis, I first try to present the most sympathetic argument for Kant's case, and then critically reflect upon it. His novel hypothesis was not quite the novelty he would have us believe.

A familiar view of the state of the problem is this: the distinctions between a priori and a posteriori, on the one hand, and analytic and synthetic, on the other, were not new. Prior to Kant, some thinkers held that some judgments were analytic and a priori, others were synthetic and a posteriori. It was agreed that there could neither be judgments analytic and a posteriori, nor synthetic and a priori. Thus, the insistence upon not merely the possibility of synthetic and a priori, but that this structure of judgment underlied the secure path of the sciences and the possibility of a science of metaphysics, was systematically novel. Indeed, this sort of a commonly held view seems to follow Kant's expressed declarations, if we are to believe his own assessment of the problem. For in the *Critique* at B19, Kant sums up the "General Problem of Pure Reason." He insists that the idea of showing how judgments could be both synthetic and a priori "has never previously been considered." But, in the very same sentence, he includes among the things "never previously . . . considered" the distinction between "analytic" and "synthetic" judgments.

How could he have not known that Leibniz distinguished in the *Monadology* between "truths of reason" and "truths of fact?"[5] How could he have been unaware of Hume's distinction between "relations of ideas" and "matters of fact" introduced in section 4 of the *Enquiry*, which he had certainly read by 1762,[6] or Locke's distinction between "trifling" and "instructive" propositions which he makes in the *Essay*, book IV, chapters 7 and 8,[7] or even Hobbes' dichotomy between "truths of universal propositions" and "truths of existential propositions?" To this extent, Kant would have us believe his originality when it was undeserved.

Part of the reason why this supposition of novelty remained familiar was not the fact that is was supposed to be sound. Rather, the synthetic a priori hypothesis was supposed novel precisely because it was so memorably mistaken. The combination of synthetical and a priori ingredients in a principle was judged to be impossible, by later reflectors such as Carnap[8] and C. I. Lewis,[9] who by agreeing that there could be no propositions of the sort that Kant envisages, helped to sustain the reputation for originality. Kant's supposed novelty was memorable because he was supposed to be hopelessly wrong.

The logical positivists whose business is what Blanshard called "Hume warmed-over," in rejecting the Kantian program, rejected the possibility of a priori science, and in this sense the search for certainty. In 1906, Lovejoy took up just this issue of Kant's supposedly revolutionary contribution to the history of metaphysics by the introduction of synthetic a priori propositions.[10] Lovejoy showed that Kant's assessment of his own tradition was so entirely incomplete and wrong-headed that it created the fiction that his contribution was more than a mere change in terminology. Not the revolutionary thinker he would wish to present, with the inclusion of Wolff's treatment of propositions along with those like Leibniz, Hume, Locke, and Hobbes, Lovejoy reveals a Kant who was either a plagiarist or unpardonably ignorant of the state of the problem.

Beck took up Lovejoy's challenge, in 1972,[11] and again in 1975,[12] followed in agreement with the general line of Lovejoy's criticism, but argued to secure an element of novelty. Kant argues for just this novel hypothesis in a letter to Reinhold in 1789.[13] He replied to the challenge by Eberhard that the problem of the *Critique of Pure Reason*, "How are synthetic *a priori* judgments possible?" had already been answered by Wolff, and that all Kant added to the matter was a new and confusing terminology. He responded to this charge, writing to Reinhold that maybe Wolff had, indeed, answered the question, "But the reason why the importance of the distinction has not been recognized seems to be that all *a priori* judgments were regarded [by Wolff] as analytic . . . so the whole point of the distinction disappeared."[14]

Unlike his predecessors, Kant envisages the distinction to rest not upon classifications of formal logic, but on an epistemological basis. As Beck put it, " . . . the problem as Kant sees it is one of epistemology . . . classifying judgments according to their grounds [*Wahrheitsgründe*] . . . . "[15] For our purposes here, Kant's novel hypothesis about synthetic a priori judgments is recast in the *Umänderung der Denkart*, in the transformation of a prevailing point of view, which consequently brought forth the demand for the conditions according to which objects conform to mind, the epistemological turn. The change in point of view forces a re-interpretation of the context of the earlier distinctions, and in this consists its novelty. Even if the basic distinctions had been entertained prior to Kant, his novel hypothesis presents a new conceptual framework, a new context, which requires a reinterpretation of the very meaning of those distinctions.

The analytic-synthetic distinction thus illuminates not so much the search for certainty explored by the sciences but rather its ampliative or elaborative potential at its very foundation, and thereby a new concern for the grounding of judgments. The foundation of a science could not be merely logical propositions, tested upon the razor's edge of the principle of contradiction, which although true were merely true in virtue of their form alone. That is, an adequate ground for knowledge cannot be merely formal, established independent of all content. For Kant, the science could not rest upon true but trivial propositions. This is because the synthetic propositions of empirical science would then be of a different order from those constituting their foundation, and the system would be saddled with something of the third-man problem, a problem from which Kant could not escape if the grounding of all synthetic judgments ultimately rested on the analytic principles of logic.[16] The refusal to reduce the propositions of natural science to logical principles displayed Kant's informative new metaphysical vision of continuity in a system between its claims and its principles.

It is as a consequence of this point of view that Kant found himself with a new problem of demonstration for which he fashioned a new device constructed from the hypothetico-deductive model. This new device—the transcendental argument—became required because, unlike Aristotle who took principles of demonstration to be themselves indemonstrable, Kant believed that principles needed demonstration. The demonstration of principles now consisted in their adequacy to account for phenomena. The novel hypothesis, by seeking to secure the epistemological constraints that we impose upon experience, undermined the similitude theory of reference; since the contents of consciousness were no longer supposed to be similar to objects external to that consciousness, which were somehow the source of those mental contents, the correspondence theory of truth was shown to be inadequate to account for our knowledge. By affirming a coherence theory of truth as the only meaningful way that truth can be conceivable by us, the truth of Kant's ultimate principles, unlike Aristotle's, consisted in their adequacy to harmonize or make intelligible those appearances. Thus, Kant found himself in the midst of rationalist and empiricist theories neither of which could accommodate or fit this change in point of view. He found himself, then, with the need to retailor a method of demonstration in which the validity of so-called factual statements rested upon the conditions of their possibility—a principle, and the principle in turn had to appeal for its own validity to the possibile experience that it has rendered intelligible.

Kant's coherence theory of truth insisted upon a homogeneous element between principles and the propositions of a system, for without it there would indeed be an insurmountable hiatus between the informative statements of a system and the principles on whose conditions their very possibility rested. He reenacts the very same strategy in the "Schematism" where he supplies a "third" thing to mediate homogenously between a priori concepts and "objects in general"—that is, experience—to which the a priori concepts must somehow apply for their validity but from which they are not derived.[17] That homogenous element, in this wider strategy, proved to be the synthetic character of the propositions. From this point of view, Kant's strategy is antireductionist, in the parlance of the traditional rationalist programs. Or stated differently, certainty was required to be more than trivial.

The analytic-synthetic distinction thus exhibits two capacities within our thinking—the true but trivial, and the (apparently) contingent—and that structure of thought finds expression in our judgments. Kant implicitly supposes that every judgment can ultimately be reduced to and thus expressed in the categorical form, and hence a substance-attribute metaphysics—the predicate of every judgment either extends the knowledge of the subject concept or it does not. If it does not, then the truth of the proposition can be determined by a mere analysis of its concept since the predicate does not extend or amplify what is already given in its subject. The judgment is proclaimed to be analytic, and it is determined to be a necessary truth, a judgment whose truth is guaranteed by an appeal to its form alone. If, on the other hand, the predicate extends the subject-concept, that is amplifies it, then no mere analysis of the concepts will suffice to determine the validity of the judgment. At best contingent, and not necessary, synthetic judgments, prior to Kant were generally supposed to extend our knowledge of a subject.

The a priori –a posteriori distinction, although not fundamentally an analysis of the semantic structure of language, has been thought to be somehow parallel. Synthetic judgments were those whose validity was supposed to make an appeal a posteriori to experience. Analytic judgments, whose truth could be ascertained by a mere inspection of the concepts related within the judgment, required no appeal to experience for their validity, and were supposed to be a priori. So, Hume, in distinguishing between relations of ideas and matters of fact, distinguishes between necessary and contingent truths, without making the analytic-synthetic distinction per se. But even when Kant writes as if Hume in principle makes the correct distinction between analytic and synthetic propositions (A764–65/B792–93), he insists that Hume denies the possibility of synthetic a priori judgments. In this case, Kant claims that Hume failed to distinguish between two kinds of synthetic judgments—(i) those belonging to the understanding that may be known a priori for objects of possible experience, and (ii) those of reason that make claims about things that can never be met with in experience. Kant accuses Hume of supposing that synthetic a priori judgments would have to be of type (ii), and thereby he claimed that there could be no synthetic a priori judgments at all. From this point of view, as Beck put it, " . . . Kant, precisely by making this distinction, did not have to condemn all *a priori* synthetic judgments but only those which claim to refer beyond experience."[18] Part of Kant's novel hypothesis, then, was effectively to extend the range of synthetic judgments, by distinguishing between two types of employment, and the two types of objects to which the judgments purportedly refer. This move was crucial because otherwise Kant would have been left with the Wolff-Leibniz program of seeking an ultimate reduction of principles to the strictures of logic, in particular, the principle of contradiction, in order to ground their validity.[19]

Thus, one side of Kant's novel hypothesis consisted in reinterpreting the range of synthetic propositions, from the transformed point of view. The other side consisted in reinterpreting the domain of the a priori, by driving a wedge between statements that were analytic and those that were a priori. Even if, as we shall go on to consider, both Wolff and Crusius took up this project, the meaning of the enterprise is different because of the change in context.[20] This seems sufficient reason to acknowledge Kant's novelty, if not his revolutionary status.

The further examination of this change in point of view, places us in a better position to appraise Kant's self-proclaimed revolutionary contribution, by examining his own novel hypothesis. The novel hypothesis is to suppose that the fundamental presuppositions of all knowledge and experience are expressed in judgments whose validity cannot be determined by mere conceptual inspection and which nevertheless do not appeal to experience whatsoever for their confirmation. Why don't they appeal to experience for their confirmation? Because they are the conditions that make experience possible in the first place. Without these suppositions a priori, Kant believes our very experience would not be possible, for the principles he ultimately advances are the very conditions of even having an experience. Science, whatever else it may be, must conform to these conditions, if it too is to be included as part of our experience.

Kant's view that the foundation of the sciences is constituted by synthetic a priori judgments proposed the commitment that a sound science must provide certainty and yet must, at the same time, enlarge our knowledge. That the propositions of a science enlarge our knowledge, that is, are ampliative, requires the synthetical form; but the requirement that such propositions be certain provided the difficulty that led Kant to rethink the possible alignment between synthetic and a priori. The analytic/a priori although offering the prospect for certitude seemed to undermine any attempt to provide ampliative propositions, for logical truths prove to be trivial as a result of their form. What Kant succeeded in doing was to drive a wedge between the analytic and the a priori. His motive for doing so follows the work of Crusius, who sought to distinguish within the class of necessary truths those that were analytic from those that although not analytic, were still necessary. Following the leads of Ralph C. S. Walker[21] and Beck,[22] we turn to investigate the class of necessary but nonanalytic judgments.

According to Leibniz, there are two first principles: the principle of contradiction, and the principle of sufficient reason. The first is called upon to distinguish necessary truths from all others; a denial of a necessary truth is a self-contradiction in terms. The second principle is appealed to in order to distinguish the truth of a posteriori or synthetical claims; the truth of every synthetical proposition requires a sufficient reason.[23] Now, for Kant to suppose that within the class of necessary truths there were judgments that were necessary but not analytic, Kant had to suppose that the foundation of systems could contain principles that were nonlogical, that is, whose truth could not be revealed by an appeal to the principle of contradiction. And so Kant finds himself with the problem of justifying these principles, for apart from the condition that the denial of certain principles is self-contradictory, what good reasons could be proposed for accepting the truth of these other principles whose denials were not self-contradictory?[24]

It is Kant's insistence upon the synthetical character of the fundamental propositions of metaphysics and science that demands a review of the nature and development of science, and this shows itself in a new task of justification, a task that is already thought through and self-contained within the novel hypothesis of synthetic a priori principles. The commitment to nonlogical first principles drives Kant to seek the grounds for accepting these propositions as true. In Kant's work, this project appears as the central thrust of the first *Critique*, an enterprise that seeks to show how synthetic a priori judgments are possible—that is, how there can be judgments that are necessarily true, but not by virtue of their logical form alone. This central thrust is the epistemological turn, and that turn is Kant's novel hypothesis on analogy with Copernicus' hypothesis of a transformation in point of view.

At the same time, this strategy makes clear the predicament of earlier philosophical defenses of science. The rationalist/reductionist program seeks to imitate the traditional method of mathematics—not natural science—which takes Euclid as its model. The certainty of the science is secured first. The ultimate principles of that science, as the reductionist program supposed, were analytic and a priori. Specific theorems were ultimately shown to be necessary consequences of tautogological expressions that were their presuppositions, and thus were supposed to be tautologous themselves. The theorems were shown to be necessarily implied by truths whose necessity was a function of their very form. Thus the theorems were ultimately revealed by the rigorous deduction to be necessary truths themselves, that is propositions analytic and a priori like the principles from which they were derived.

This strategy naturally proved more complicated when applied to empirical objects. The problem of reducing a posteriori claims to principles whose truth was secured by their form alone was met with two strategies. The rationalist strategy was to reject the a posteriori dimension as a genuine candidate for knowledge, since the rationalist strategy understands that the required reduction cannot be achieved while still escaping the charge of artificiality. The rationalists in seeing the hopelessness of trying to reduce synthetical propositions to their ultimate logical grounds, dismissed the synthetical claims as fundamentally unknowable and thereby not a part of knowledge as such. The empiricist strategy was to refuse to grant an a priori and thereby absolutely certain status to the principles. They too saw that the reduction could not be carried out, and thus a system could not be justified, if it took seriously a posteriori claims and yet insisted that the validity of these claims ultimately rests upon tautologous analytic principles. Their response, however, was to reject the idea that the ultimate principles of knowledge were analytic. The rationalist gets certainty at the price of dismissing the theoretical meaningfulness of experience. The empiricist gets the meaningfulness of experience at the price of scepticism.

Both the rationalist and empiricist strategy shared the same diagnosis of the epistemological dilemma: one cannot take seriously the a posteriori dimension of experience and still consistently maintain that the ultimate principles of knowledge were analytic, whose validity consisted in an appeal to the principle of contradiction. From logical first principles, there arises an insurmountable hiatus to the nonlogical judgments that comprise the body of a science. The synthetical or ampliative judgments that constitute the body of a science enlarge our knowledge and cannot be reduced to analytic propositions, that are trivially true, which supposedly function as ultimate principles. Kant proposes a bridge to conjoin the demand for a fundamental principle sufficiently robust to enlarge our knowledge and sufficiently independent of all experience so that it can never be undermined by any future experience and thereby capable of providing the guarantee of certainty. The insistence upon the synthetical character of a class of necessary truths provided just the bridge for overcoming that hiatus, if only Kant could convincingly show how such judgments could be possible.

Kant's strategy, it is worthy of note, has a peculiar nonreductive feature,[25] and in this consists part of its novelty. The Leibnizian and boldly rational project of reducing all mathematical and empirical judgments, ultimately, to higher principles—usually logical—is here abandoned. Kant's teacher Wolff, who edits and integrates the Leibnizian project, as Ralph Walker has shown,[26] lacking the logical treatises that outline Leibniz' insistence upon both the principle of contradiction and the principle of sufficient reason, attempted to reduce all judgments and principles to the principle of contradiction. Wolff's maneuver represents a strong reductionistic program, to ground all empirical judgments ultimately upon logical principles.

The motive for such a strategy reflects the requirement to supply an ultimate grounding. Why accept the judgments of some system or other? The rationalist answer was because the ultimate guidance for validity is expressed—even if it must be negatively—in a minimal condition for meaningfulness. Judgments that are self-contradictory can have no meaning; they have no meaning because they are incapable of referring to any object whatsoever. The minimal condition for reference is that a statement must be capable of referring to an object, and that condition is vitiated when one utters a contradiction. Kant extends his nonreductionistic strategy to develop the rationalist ideal of a minimal condition for meaning: a judgment must refer to a possible object of experience in order to have meaning. For Kant, this means that principles must be applied to the contents of intuition, and thus have a touchstone in sensation in order to be objectively valid.[27] The rationalist-reductionistic project makes no provision for this sort of meaning.

To make this point clearer, it need be added that Kant's treatment of mathematics reflects just this nonreductionistic strategy. If a propositions' meaningfulness consists in its ability to refer to possible objects of experience, and the judgments of logic fail to meet this condition, since they are entirely empty of content, then the treatment of mathematical judgments, if they are to be meaningful—from a strategic point of view—cannot be reduced to the status of logical judgments, by supporting some sort of reduction to the principle of contradiction.

Kant's insistence that mathematical judgments, one and all, are synthetic makes this strategic move clear.[28] The insistence upon the synthetic character of mathematical propositions warns against even the attempt at any reductionistic maneuver to logical first principles. At the same time, the strategy insists upon something of an existential character of mathematical propositions, since in order to be meaningful they must be capable of referring to possible objects of experience, and unlike the judgments of logic, they do, for Kant, have this capacity for reference.[29]

Thus the enterprise of securing a foundation for metaphysics rests on showing that metaphysics is a science. Despite Kant's insistence that the specific laws in the sciences can only be determined by an empirical investigation, that is, a posteriori, Kant presumes, first of all, that a genuine science is set upon a foundation unassailable by future experience—and in this sense certain—precisely because it makes no appeal to experience for its validity in the first place. Such a strategic maneuver is designed to ensure certainty and thereby undermine what Kant accepted as the most forceful sceptical challenge, that science could at best provide probable explanation.

Secondly, the insistence upon the synthetic character of the fundamental judgments of a science displays the antireductionist strategy, which commits Kant, not only to an ampliative ideal of science, but also one where meaning is grounded upon the capacity for reference. Insisting that the highest principles of all science were nonlogical judgements avoided the dilemma of the so-called third-man arguments. For if the validity of empirical judgments ultimately rests upon nonempirical judgments—since the empirical character of the judgments required a defense—then one must show how the nonempirical judgments can ground the empirical that are judgments of a different order. If the validity of empirical judgments rests ultimately upon nonempirical judgments that nonetheless share the synthetical character, the enterprise has been transformed, but at a price. Now, a new kind of demonstration will be required in order to ground the fundamental principles of science, which cannot have the structure of logical deductions, whose procedure is useful for those sub-scribing to a reductionistic strategy. The deduction of the highest princi-ples, which are at once synthetical, reveals a new formulation about the ultimate ground of knowledge, and poses a new problem of demonstra-tion. To articulate the dimensions of that problem finally exhibits Kant's purported revolution in philosophy: Kant's Newtonian revolution in phi-losophy. If anything in Kant's project deserves to be called revolution-ary it is the interpretation and application of this novel method of demonstration.

Kant's Newtonian Revolution: Transcendental Arguments and the Requirement of Demonstration in the *Critique*

9.A. Kant's Problem of Demonstration in General

A PROOF OR DEMONSTRATION OF KANT'S NOVEL HYPOTHESIS—THAT THE fundamental judgments to which any meaningful claim to knowledge must refer are synthetic a priori—is offered in the transcendental analytic of the *Critique*. Any claim to knowledge is shown to be valid insofar as we can point to the principle that is the condition of its possibility; and the principle is valid only for the possible experience that it illuminates. Kant believes that the proof he offers is apodeictic. If this is so, then by both the estimations of Wolff's and Kant's program, the novel hypothesis proved to be true and not false/imaginary.

The proof has two general stages, following the twofold strategy outlined in Newton's *Opticks:* (a) a metaphysical deduction or deduction *quid facti* and (b) a transcendental deduction or deduction *quid juris*. The metaphysical deduction exhibits the a priori structures presupposed by the entire range of multifarious experience; the transcendental deduction shows that these a priori structures are necessary, but that validity is restricted to that experience only. In that transcendental deduction, Kant works out the consequences of his novel hypothesis in such a way as to show that the proofs for an external world independent of the contents of consciousness, and of a self to which one and all of our experiences may be properly referred, are inescapable facts which follow from our sensible intuition: if there were nothing outside of and independent of our consciousness we would never become self-conscious. Our experience of self-consciousness, although a transcendental condition that must be presupposed in order to account for the synthetic activity of our understanding, would never emerge in experience were it not for something external that started internal activity. This is because, radically revising the rationalist conclusion, the self—as an object of theoretical knowledge—is not a substance, it is an activity. Our fundamental theoretical identity is our synthesizing activity, whose a priori structures account for the experience we in fact have.

Kant's *quid facti* argument bears some resemblance to Aristotle's *hoti* argument, and the argument *quia* in Galileo. The similarity is that these arguments claim to set out the fact of the matter, the facts of each case. The other argument, *quid juris*, an argument for the legitimacy or justification of those facts, is not parallel to Galileo's *propter quid* argument, or Aristotle's *dioti*. It is at this final stage that we discover Kant's innovation for metaphysics, for it is here that Kant displays how the method of deduction or synthesis can be accommodated to the queen of the sciences.[4]

Kant's argument *quid juris* claims to demonstrate the principles underlying all meaningful theoretical knowledge, and claims to articulate the very conditions that must be presupposed a priori without which we could not have the experience that, indeed, we do have. Each stage has its own difficulties, but the demonstration *quid juris* is intended to provide the ultimate grounding. Its purpose is to demonstrate the supposedly revolutionary consequences of the epistemological turn, and achieves whatever measure of success by means of a transcendental argument. I turn first to examine difficulties concerning Kant's project of the deduction *quid facti* —and to this extent a review of the status of the Aristotelian dimension of Kant's project—and then finally turn to the deduction *quid juris*.

I argue that the demonstration *quid facti*, although perhaps entirely novel is highly dubious. That Kant should have believed he had isolated the a priori structure of cognition, the details of his God's eye point of view, by this unargumentative extravaganza, strikes this thinker as the most disappointing part of the *Critique*. Without the slightest argument, Kant believes he can take the guidance of traditional logic to isolate the categorial presuppositions of meaningful experience. Then, notwithstanding this objection, I show that the constraints on deduction forced Kant to adapt Newton's method, as a consequence of his novel hypothesis. The result was the employment of a new logical technique, for bridging the a priori structure of our reason with the contents of experience, which Wolff called the marriage of reason and experience. The new logical bridge proves to be a conjectural method for meeting the sceptical challenge. The challenge forces Kant to a startling revelation that the most immediate awareness we have is nevertheless not obvious or evident, and so requires a demonstration. Despite his insistence to the contrary, there is no way to accommodate this maneuver within an Aristotelian world view.

The curious dilemma of demanding a demonstration of the immediate but not evident awakened Kant to a conundrum of reason. That although reason has insight only into that which it produces after a plan of its own, evidently reason is in the predicament of knowing without knowing that it knows. In the "Refutation of Idealism," Kant tries to work out the consequence of the deduction *quid juris*, the transcendental deduction of the categories, by showing that (1) the necessary supposition of the unity of consciousness—the condition without which we could not have the experience that we in fact have—is possible only on (2) the supposition of an immediate consciousness of external objects. The argument is designed to bridge the a priori dimension of experience with the sensible intuition to which it must apply, if it is to be valid, by simultaneously offering a constructive response to the sceptic who claims that there can be no meaningful demonstration of a reference of an "I" that underlies diverse experiences, and there is no world that can be demonstrated to be independent of my representation of it. Kant's refutation of Berkeley shows—granting Berkeley's collapse of Locke's distinction between primary and secondary qualities, and thereby the subjective idealism to which he succumbs—that an examination of the contents of consciousness reveals an ingredient that cannot be reduced to other mental states. Berkeley's argument leads to the conclusion that one can never escape from the contents of consciousness; Kant agrees but shows that an examination of just those contents is sufficient to prove that the experience of those mental contents would be impossible were it not for an ingredient supplied external to that consciousness: this is Kant's peculiar discovery of the given.

The dilemma of reason is that it must uncover its own condition, it must reveal to itself its own nature and plan. Kant's novel hypothesis called for a new theory of demonstration, the process by which reason comes to know what it already knows, a process by which reason puts itself on *der sichere Gang einer Wissenschaft*, "the secure path of a science." To demonstrate this process in such a way as to show that without this supposed structure we could not account for the very experience that we indeed do have, would be, in Kant's estimation, to demonstrate the science of metaphysics.

9.B. Demonstration *Quid Facti* and the Irrational Knowledge of the Rational

The fundamental principles of science are what Kant calls the schematized categories: the principles. Kant believes them to be presupposed by Newtonian natural science and are the foundations of a constructive theoretical metaphysics. Although the ultimate principles of the schematized categories must ultimately conform to the highest principles of all analytic and synthetic judgments, such a conformity is negative and minimal only. The principle of contradiction, Kant holds, is the highest principle of all analytic judgments.[2] He declares that a minimal condition for meaningfulness consists in a judgment's capacity to refer and that capacity is effectively undermined if a judgment contains a self-contradiction.

Meaning and reference also underscore Kant's articulation of the highest principle of all synthetic judgments, which is not the principle of sufficient reason. Rather, it maintains that "every object stands under the necessary conditions of synthetic unity of the manifold of intuition in a possible experience" (A158/B197). Indeed, the highest principle of all synthetic judgments is the issue before us. In short, the claim amounts to this. Every meaningful object must conform to the conditions—a priori—that we impose upon experience, in order to be an object of experience, for if they did not conform, they could not be an object of our experience. Those conditions include not only the conceptual conditions we bring to sensations and thereby with which we structure those sensations, but also include, or rather demand, the application of this a priori conceptual apparatus to the contents of empirical intuition, and hence can refer only by finding application to that intuition. Thus, in order to make a meaningful judgment, and hence to refer to an object, the conceptual organization is valid only for and by virtue of this connection to sensation. The highest principle of synthetic judgments explicates the nature of being a meaningful object. Thus, the principles of science operate within the constraint that the vehicles of ultimate meaning are the ultimate conditions of meaningful objects, and they find expression in synthetic a priori judgments.[3]

The articulation of these highest principles follows within the architectonic of the critical enterprise. In the "Transcendental Aesthetic," Kant sought to set out the a priori conditions that underlie the very possibility of having perceptions. Interestingly enough, his conclusion committed him to the view that the structure of mathematical awareness is identical with the structure of perceptual awareness. Hence, by demonstrating the conditions for the possibility of perception, Kant was at the same time demonstrating the conditions that made mathematics possible, for both perception and mathematics share the same constructive structure.

That demonstration consisted in showing the a priori conditions that made perception (equals aesthetic) or mathematics possible. Those a priori conditions proved to be that space and time were the forms of all our intuition. In order to have perceptual experience, a necessary condition that must be supposed as a condition for its very possibility is that all our intuition is sensible. The sensations we receive, one and all, are conditioned by space and time, conditions that we impose upon experience.[4] If Kant can show that space and time are a priori forms of perceptual awareness—because he can show that space and time are a priori—then at once the status of mathematics as a science is revealed.

Since he has insisted that mathematical propositions are synthetic, and since he believes that mathematics is constituted of two enterprises, geometry whose judgments are about space and arithmetic whose judgments are about succession which he equates with time, then if he can show that space and time are a priori, he believes that he accomplishes the objective of demonstrating that mathematics is a science since its propositions are synthetic and are a priori so far as they characterize the form of intuition. Hence, the enterprise of demonstrating mathematics to be a science is one and the same with demonstrating the scientific dimension of our perceptual awareness. The objective validity of the science of mathematics shares the very same objective validity of perception, since science for Kant ultimately rests upon the "laws of nature" which we legislate and prescribe to experience. As he puts it, "however exaggerated and absurd it may sound" (A127).

The conditions of perceptual and mathematical awareness, Kant articulates within the discussion of the faculty of sensibility. The distinction insisted upon here, between sensibility, the receptive or passive faculty, and the understanding, the active or spontaneous faculty, follows the lines of the antireductionist strategy. The hiatus between these two faculties must be bridged,[5] and critics have long sought to show that even if one accepts Kant's project, the bridge he proposes is unconvincing or wrong-headed.[6] In Kant's design, bridging the hiatus between the passive and active—by way of the imagination, which seems to have an anchoring to each domain (although this is far from clear)[7]—Kant refuses to permit one domain to collapse into the other. The understanding must operate upon something given, independent of its own control; hence, "all knowledge begins with experience" (B1). But, although all knowledge begins with experience, "it does not follow that it all arises from experience" (B1); the contents of intuition, structured by sensibility, must be comprehended through the employment of the understanding whose categories are a priori—they are neither derived nor abstracted from the experience with which all knowledge begins. Thus, the antireductionist strategy requires a separate treatment of the conditions for intuition, which amounts to the innate structure of perceptual and mathematical awareness, on the one hand, and the innate structure of comprehension of the contents of this awareness, on the other. The investigations, however, are to be kept separate. In combination, the innate or a priori structures we bring to and impose upon experience; and it is to these conditions that experience must conform, if it is to be an experience for us, creatures whose intuition can only be sensible.

The problem of the deduction *quid facti* reveals its complexity in Kant's *Critique* once the nature of the understanding is explored. The exploration reveals the following. First, Kant examines the structure of comprehension by turning his attention to the structure of judgments. A judgment exhibits a connection of and in a sensible manifold; a judgment expresses something already comprehended. Every judgment presents a connection of concepts, and those concepts by and large are derived or abstracted from experience. The important point to be kept in mind is that Kant's coherence theory of truth commits him to the view that awareness or self-consciousness is identical to the act of judging.

The judgment "The cat is gray" expresses something comprehended. To comprehend is to organize the sensible manifold—the intuition—under concepts. The judgment "The cat is gray" reflects the judging already accomplished: within a manifold of sense impressions, I have organized that intuition in such a way that not only is a subject of those impressions discerned (i.e., "cat") and a characteristic or property (i.e., "gray") has been grasped, but also that there is a "subject"—cat—and a "property"—gray—organized in such a way that I grasp that "gray" belongs to "cat" and not vice versa. In addition to the employment of empirical concepts in judgments, there is a structure of organization that is expressed in the judgment, and that structure is exposed in its logical form. That logical structure—the science of logic—Kant suggests, has been exhaustively grasped as early as the writing of Aristotle's logic.

Kant had already gone so far as to say in the opening of the Preface to the second edition, "That logic has already, from the earliest times, proceeded upon this sure path is evidenced by the fact that since Aristotle it has not been required to retrace a single step . . ." (Bvii). What this means for Kant's task is that the logical forms of judgment, which reveal the structure of all comprehension for creatures with sensible intuitions, is already completely and exhaustively provided. Kant, then, constructs a table of all the logical forms of judgments, suggests that the logical forms of judgment are expressions of innate mental operations that give rise to it, and thus believes he can read—quite directly from this long-accepted and satisfactorily delineated table of judgments—the principles of the mental operations—the categories—which exhibit this structure of comprehension.

Kant sets out the table of categories, corresponding to the table of judgments, declaring the enterprise an "exhaustive inventory" of the powers of the understanding,[8] and identifying his "primary purpose" to be the "same" as Aristotle's, "although widely diverging in its manner of execution" (B105). To say that his purpose is the same but the manner of execution diverges widely only succeeds in obfuscating what Kant seeks to demonstrate and how that demonstration proceeds.

This much is clear at the outset. Kant believes that there is a certain logical structure to our experience, and that, in fact, certain kinds of concepts show themselves in experience. Of course, Kant wants to insist that innate or a priori concepts must indeed show themselves in experience, and more than that, he must show that these concepts are necessary for without them there would be no experience at all. But the mode of demonstration begins with the so-called metaphysical deduction in which *quid facti* Kant wants to show that we, in fact, do make use of a priori concepts—or categories—because the fact of the matter, it so happens, is that the exhaustive study of logical forms of judgment reveals the finite list, the twelve categories, of principles of mental organization that give rise to and are presupposed by the exhaustive account of the logical forms of thought.

When that has been accomplished, Kant proceeds to the argument *quid juris* for the legitimacy of the employment of categories—that the employment is necessary. This is most clearly the stage where Kant parts company from Aristotle. The trouble with this sort of demonstrative strategy is that, the method of revealing logic and its character—since Kant is ever concerned to insist that the validity of the a priori structure of human understanding requires that we show its application in experience—proves unable to divorce itself from an empirical character.[9] As Hegel rightly put it: "In the usual logical treatises various divisions and kinds of concepts occur. It is immediately obvious that it is inconsequent to introduce the kinds like this: there are the following kinds of quantity, the following kinds of quality, etc. This gives no other justification than these kinds occur and show themselves in experience. We arrive in this way at an empirical logic—a strange science, irrational knowledge of the rational."[10]

For whatever else Aristotle's logic sought to show, the necessary application of principles to experience as a condition for their own validity was not one of them. As a result, the method of demonstration operated within very different constraints. The conditions for a demonstration of the reasoned fact, what the medieval and renaissance logicians tended to call a *propter quid* argument, and what Aristotle calls a *dioti* argument to distinguish it from the nondemonstrative argument called the *hoti*, never began with the primacy of experience and required that the validity of the logic rested upon the application in experience. And so, it is extremely misleading for Kant to suppose that he makes no contribution to the traditional logic, taking it from the ancients without retracing a single step. To say his manner of execution, alone, separates his enterprise from that of Aristotle is far too much of an understatement, for the manner of execution radically reinterprets the status of logic, the idea of a demonstration, and thereby the demonstrative character of anything deserving to be called a science.

If Hegel's suspicion is right, as Gottfried Martin had also supposed in his *Kant's Metaphysics and Theory of Science*,[11] that Kant provides at best an "empirical logic," and thus the categories and the synthetic unity supposed by the employment of the categories must at best share that "empirical" character, then Kant's enterprise proves to advance a "strange science," an "irrational knowledge of the rational." The character of demonstration, because of the required connection to the empirical elements in experience, is the methodological key to a new vision of the nature of a science of metaphysics. Not only does Kant ultimately abandon Aristotle and the traditional logical project, he does so by reinterpreting the world that logic seeks to connect by attempting to reconnect the world in a new way: this is another way of describing his novel hypothesis. That new way, or critical philosophy, is expressed in and through the method of demonstration. Hence, the novel hypothesis consists in both a specific claim and a demonstration of that claim, which itself is an illustration of it. Kant's novel hypothesis thus proves to be about novel hypotheses and their demonstrations, as well as being one itself. The hypothesis about hypotheses must itself secure a rigorous demonstration, yielding established certainty. Otherwise, it would reveal itself, as Wolff had warned, and Kant evidentally agreed, to be false and imaginary.

9.C. Deduction *Quid Juris*:
The Logic of Demonstrating the Immediate

Unfortunately what is self-evident is not obvious to everyone.
—*Arthur Schopenhauer, discussing Kant, in the World as Will and Representation*

9.C.1. A Brief Reflection on Demonstration
in Aristotle's *Posterior Analytics*

Aristotle, in book 1, chapter 2 of the *Posterior Analytics* distinguishes between two principles of demonstration, a thesis or posit and an axiom (72b15ff.), a distinction that he later describes between common and proper principles (76a37–b2). In both cases the principles are indemonstrable (*anapodeiktos*, 71b28).[12] In the case of posits, we have principles that cannot be proved " . . . .but it is not necessary for anyone who is to learn anything to grasp it." In the case of axioms we have principles that also cannot be proved but of which " . . . it is necessary for anyone who is going to learn anything whatever to grasp" (72a15–19).

Thus, all demonstration (*apodeixis*) supposes an ultimate foundation that is not itself demonstrated. When the question for justification is raised for a particular claim, appeals are made to principles that are not themselves proven. Thus the principles are, says Aristotle, "true," "primitive," "immediate," "more familiar than and prior to and explanatory of the conclusion" demonstrated, and the principles themselves must be "indemonstrable."

"Deduction" (*sullogismos*) can take place without these conditions being met, but "there will not be demonstration" (*apodeixis*) (71b24–25). Thus, two points stand out in Aristotle's theory of demonstration: (1) demonstration is more than a deduction, since it supplies an appeal to principles that "produce understanding" (71b25). Aristotle insists that demonstration provides an "explanation and the reason why" (85b27–28),[13] and thus reveals the essential nature of a thing. Hence, a demonstration is required for propositions that are neither immediate nor obvious. The demonstration supplies the necessary evidence or justification. And (2) demonstration justifies a proposition, ultimately, by an appeal to principles that cannot be justified. Hence not only self-evident, obvious, and immediate, principles are of a different kind from the theorems from which they are deduced. The principles are the necessary presuppositions for understanding without themselves being capable of demonstration, and this is on account of their immediateness.

The discovery of first principles Aristotle considers in the celebrated and widely disputed chapter 19 of book 2 of the *Posterior Analytics*. There, it seems, Aristotle argues that the indemonstrable first principles are grasped by *epagoge* or "induction," on the one hand, or *nous*, "intuition," on the other. There is no reason to debate that important doctrine here since the crucial point for my purpose is to make clear that the principles are neither capable nor in need of demonstration, regardless of how they are discovered.

For Kant, the argument *quid facti* roughly parallels what Galileo calls the demonstration *quia*, and what Aristotle calls the "argument to fact" (*hoti*, 78b35). But, the argument *quid juris* in the first *Critique* has no parallel with Aristotle's "argument for the reasoned fact" (*dioti*, 75b35) or Galileo's argument *propter quid*. As Galileo turned to develop the demonstrative regress to accommodate a problem, tied to an empirical grounding of experience, so Kant introduces, develops, and exploits an argument form that, not accurately a deduction since it involves a twofold regressus, is a demonstration of legitimacy, a demonstration of the conditions without which demonstration and, moreover, all experience itself would be impossible. This enterprise constitutes Kant's application of his novel hypothesis to the logic of demonstration. The logical innovation—despite his unwillingness to see it in this fashion—is perhaps his greatest claim to effect a revolution in philosophy.

Galileo was led to pursue a novel hypothesis with regard to the logic of demonstration because the empirical component of hypothesis-making required that one be able to infer not only the conclusion from the premises but also the premises from the conclusion. Beginning with experience—observations—Galileo sought to justify an inference to the conditions of its possibility—causes—that are presented in the premises in every rigorous, demonstrative *propter quid* argument. As every rigorous argument shows that the claim in the conclusion is a necessary consequent of the premises, Galileo believed a twofold *progressus* could be validly formulated. Inferring premises from the conclusion and conclusion from premises is justified on the supposition that there is a deeper connection between the deduction of the conclusion and the inference from conclusion to premises based on an appeal to experience. That connection, in Kant's estimation, is the supposed necessary relation between the a priori structure of our reasoning and the sensible contents of our intuition.[14]

Kant is committed to an epistemological vision whereby the a priori structure of knowing is valid only for objects of possible experience. The meaning of the a priori status of our knowledge is one that must find application to the contents of sensible intuition, if we are to have knowledge. The project to ground all judgments on principles both a priori and synthetic is another way of expressing the requirement of bridging the hiatus between a certain and yet ampliative nature of a science, metaphysics among the sciences.

9.C.2. Demonstration *Quid Juris* in the "Transcendental Deduction"

In the "Metaphysical Deduction," Kant follows the procedure of method as it is described in the closing passages of Newton's *Opticks*. Having granted the given—sensible experience—Kant believes himself to be setting out the most general structures of comprehension that are presupposed in all of our knowing. This method Newton describes as the goal of analysis or induction: the method is to proceed "from effects to their causes, and from particular causes to more general ones til the argument end in the most general." The end of the method of analysis is the presentation of the fundamental and exhaustive table of categories presupposed by that judgmental structure that found exhaustive expression in the table of judgments. The fact of the matter is that we indeed use categories, in Kant's estimation, in the process of knowing.

In the "Transcendental Deduction" Kant follows the method that Newton calls synthesis or deduction: the method "consists in assuming the causes discovered, and established as principles, and by them explaining the phenomena proceeding from them and proving the explanations."[15] In Kant's project, the method of synthesis is accommodated to metaphysics so that the structures or categorial principles are shown to be adequate to that given experience. The method is to show that the given experiences can be accounted for only on the condition of the categorial structure. In a word, the method is intended to show that the categories are necessary—not absolutely, but only for the sensible-experience they are intended to make intelligible. In this sense, Kant's demonstration follows the programmatic commitment to a coherence theory of truth.

In order to show that the employment of categories is legitimate, and that is because their employment is necessary for knowledge, Kant finds himself looking beyond the categories as such. The categories express those mental operations, employed by creatures like ourselves with sensible intuition, whose operations find expression in the structure of judgments to which they give rise. In order to account for this phenomenon, Kant isolates two consequences that turn out, upon further scrutiny, to be presuppositions for the employment of these operations: (1) the unity of consciousness, which is not a thing but a transcendental condition and an activity, and (2) an external world without which self-consciousness would be impossible.

First, self-consciousness. His argument turns on the recognition that these operations of synthesizing the manifold of sense impressions presuppose a source of these syntheses: this is the unity of apperception, the unity of consciousness, which enables me to say that one and all of the representations I have are mine. This unity of consciousness is both a transcendental condition, which must be presupposed to account for the having of experience in the first place, since the experience must be someone's, and it is an activity the consciousness of which arises from the synthetic reworking of the manifold of sensations.

Secondly, the external world. Having come to realize that the self that I can know theoretically is both a condition and activity, Kant discovers that consciousness of self presupposes a source that generates the activity, since it itself is not a substance. As an activity, it operates upon something given. That source is the given sensations, outside and independent of my control that somehow are the source of my representations, although they do not bear a similarity to their source in a corresponding sense. Kant is led to embrace a theory that matter is active; my very having of sensations has its source in active-matter.

The connection between these two essential ingredients of Kant's adaptation of Newton's expressed method is this. The proof that there indeed is an external world rests upon my recognition that the self is not a substance but the source of the syntheses whose categorial structures find expression in the logical form of judgments that we in fact employ. Locke attempted to argue for the existence of an external world by distinguishing between two ideas whose power he believed to be qualities in the object. Primary, or mind-independent, qualities he believed could be distinguished from secondary or mind-dependent qualities. My idea of extension, for instance, is a power that I can attribute to the object independently of my grasping of it; color on the other hand is not in the object per se but a subjective description about which there may always be great disagreement. Berkeley criticized Locke by insisting that our experience of extension is always accompanied by color; in general, primary qualities are never experienced in isolation from secondary qualities, and thus so-called mind-independent qualities are never experienced independent of the mind-dependent ones. And if our experience cannot separate out primary and secondary, then the distinction collapses. The result is that we cannot succeed in arguing for qualities that reside in the object independent of our conscious—and thereby subjective—states. Berkeley criticized Locke for supposing that he could infer from the contents of consciousness the existence of objects independent of that consciousness. How could he achieve this justifiably? There is no way to climb outside one's own consciousness and check if there are objects that somehow correspond independent of that consciousness. Kant grants Berkeley's critique of Locke, but insists that Berkeley himself made an error.

Kant's insight was to grasp that an inspection of the contents of consciousness is sufficient to reveal that there is an ingredient that cannot be reduced to other conscious states. This was Kant's discovery of the given—the touchstone in sensation, the required grounding in experience. Agreeing with Berkeley that there is no way to climb outside of our heads and check to see if the world corresponds to the contents of our consciousness, Kant is satisfied to insist that if there were no external world—and thus no given sensations whose source was active matter— one would never have the experience of self-consciousness. But we do have the experience of self-consciousness; therefore there must be an external world that provides the given sensations that start the sensible-intuiting machine of cognition. Let us examine this structure more fully.

The structure of transcendental arguments is unlike that of deductive arguments in general. In 1968, Stroud offered the following assessment:

> Kant thought that his transcendental proofs counted in a unique way against both scepticism and conventionalism because their conclusions were synthetic and could be known *a priori*. They are shown to have this status by a transcendental argument which proves that the truth of its conclusion is a necessary condition of there being any experience or thought at all. If the conclusion were not true, there could be no experience to falsify it. For Kant, proofs that such-and-such is a necessary condition of thought or experience in general therefore have a special feature which is not shared by other proofs that one thing is a necessary condition of another, and because they have this feature they can answer the "question of justification."[16]

The structure of the transcendental argument, then, seeks to reveal the necessary conditions for having an experience at all. [17] In the transcendental deduction, there seem to be two levels of argument. The first level attempts to demonstrate that the use of categories is necessary, that without them we could not account for the experience we have. The second level seeks to show the necessary employment of categories presupposes a unity of consciousness and an external world. The unity of consciousness is both a transcendental condition—the transcendental unity of apperception, the necessary presupposition for having an experience is that the experience can be referred to a consciousness that is having it—and a synthetic unity of apperception—the self-consciousness that arises from the synthetic reworking of the manifold in intuition. The condition that must be supposed in order to account for this self-consciousness is the existence of a world of active matter independent of my consciousness.

The first level transcendental argument attempts to demonstrate that the use of categories is necessary. For instance, the experience of an event is made possible on the supposition, not that we abstract from empirical consciousness to discover causality but, that we come to discover that we have imposed the principle of causality a priori upon experience. Kant agrees with Hume that causality would be a mere illusion if one supposed it to be an empirical abstraction from sensations. But, from the fact that we have no sense impression of causal connection, Hume was not entitled to conclude that there is no causal connection. Hume failed effectively to consider that it is we who, a priori, bring causality to experience. Casuality is a character of our self-imposing[18] conditions upon possible experience, and it is not derived from it.

When Kant reflects on the schematized category of causality, he is reflecting upon a principle. For Aristotle, a principle is indemonstrable; it is incapable of proof because it is not in need of one—it is immediate, obvious, or self-evident, which Aristotle calls "primitive" (*ek proton*, 71b27). In contradistinction to Aristotle, of the principle of causality Kant says this:

> Thus no one can acquire insight into the proposition that "everything which happens has its cause," merely from concepts involved. It is not, therefore, a dogma, although from another point of view, namely from that of the sole field of its possible employment, that is, experience, it can be proved with complete apodeictic certainty. But, though it needs proof, it should be entitled a *principle*, not a theorem, because it has the peculiar character that it makes possible the very experience which is its own ground of proof, and that in this experience it must always itself be presupposed. (A737.)

The fundamental presuppositions of experience, it so happens, although immediate are not obvious, and so need a demonstration both to reveal the principles and show how they underlie experience. Thus, the principles are not only capable of proof, but in need of proof. The proof of a principle consists in demonstrating its application to experience. The principle must be shown to be a condition without which the experience we indeed have would be impossible. This strategy is dictated by the coherence theory of truth.

In the transcendental deduction, the argument proceeds first by supposing that our experiences are serial, and the series of experiences are ordered in time. Now, if someone is to be aware that the experiences are his, one must be able to distinguish oneself from those experiences and other things in general. For Kant, this amounts to the ability to apply the concept of objects,[19] to impose conditions upon the sensible content of our experience by virtue of which one can distinguish oneself from the contents of those experiences—in a word, to employ categories. Thus, the transcendental argument requires that, in employing categories, which are indeed concepts of objects, we must thereby regard an element in our experience as external to ourselves, external to the consciousness that has those represented contents. Otherwise, the argument could not proceed past the contents of consciousness. Stranded in the hopelessness of subjective idealism, our experience could never demonstrate the existence of anything but the representations themselves, the contents of consciousness. Kant would then have in no way answered the sceptical or conventionalist challenge, which is to show that we can demonstrate an external world of objects, and a self-consciousness to which the experiences of that external world can be referred.

In our experience, according to Kant, we do indeed distinguish ourselves from the contents of consciousness, but this could only be possible if our experience is structured in such a way that objects can be distinguished from the subject to which those objects are referred. Now, since we do indeed have this experience, we must be employing cognitive patterns of organization—categories—that structure the experience of objects. But, over and against the employment of patterns of organization that synthesize a sensible manifold, there is a consciousness that employs these syntheses, a consciousness that is the source of these syntheses. When the argument brings together the unity of consciousness—the condition for the possibility of experience—with the claim for the recognition of an external world that is inextricably bound to that self-consciousness, we are at the intersection of what I am referring to as the second level of the deduction.

In the transcendental deduction, the second-level demonstration points to the unity of self-consciousness as the necessary presupposition for the employment even of those principles (i.e., the categories). The problem is more complex here. The transcendental analytic attempts to show that meaningful claims to theoretical knowledge require both sensibility and understanding. The status of self-consciousness thus at once becomes problematic. For if self-consciousness is a transcendental condition, a condition for the very possibility of employing categories, then the categories cannot be applied to this transcedental unity of self-consciousness in order to yield theoretical knowledge. And yet, the transcendental deduction seeks to show that only upon the necessary condition of the unity of self-consciousness is experience possible, and hence theoretical knowledge. Thus, everything that can be known theoretically ultimately rests upon a principle, the unity of self-consciousness—which itself cannot be theoretically known, but curiously enough can and must be demonstrated.

The problem is to make sense out of the ultimate condition for the possibility of experience of which nonetheless we can have no theoretical knowledge. For Kant, the self is not a Cartesian substance; it is both a transcendental condition and an activity.[20] Patricia Kitcher has made an excellent case for the view that Kant understands the unity of self-consciousness as a "contentual dependence" of one mental state upon another, or as an "existential dependence" of one mental state upon another.[21] For, since the self is not a substance or thing, one must account for the phenomenon of activity within the unified manifold. The self is not something to be distinguished over and against the manifold of experience.

Hume denied the relation of existential dependence among mental states. Kant's reply is to insist that one and all mental states belong to an "I think," that is, can be referred as belonging to one and the same consciousness. That same consciousness amounts to a contentually interconnected system of mental states. Thus, in showing the conditions for the synthetic unity of the manifold—the first-level transcendental argument—Kant was at the same time providing what I have been speaking of as a second-level transcendental argument; the two arguments are inextricably interconnected,[22] separated here to indicate that two distinct demonstrations were required, even if Kant envisages them as inextricably tied.

Kant defines synthesis as "the act of putting different representations together, and of grasping what is manifold in them in one cognition" (A77/B103). The act of putting together representations is to combine the contents of one mental state in a further mental state, and in such a way that the further mental state could be what it is only by virtue of the preceding mental states. The contents of the further or subsequent mental state is in fact synthesized, or produced from, the earlier mental states. In this sense, the mental states are contentually dependent; the content of one mental state is dependent upon the previous mental states, and without them could not arise.[23]

In the B deduction Kant insists that representations can belong to a self " . . . not simply by accompanying each representation with consciousness, but only in so far as I conjoin one representation with another . . . [hence] the synthetic unity of the manifold of intuitions, as given a priori, is thus the ground of the identity of apperception itself" (B133,

134). The unity of consciousness thus finds expression in the contentual dependence of mental states, that is, the conjoining of one representation with another; or stated differently, in their existential dependence. The transcendental argument amounts to the claim that without this connection among representations, the representations would be representations of nothing (A116). Hence, a representation has content by comprehending other mental states, under it, because only in this way can it display the synthetic unity of consciousness.

This description of contentual dependence helps us see how the two levels of argument are bound together. Without the ability to distinguish oneself from the mere contents of consciousness, experience would not be possible for us. But, we can, and indeed must so distinguish the one from the other—without at the same time supposing that the consciousness of self is the consciousness of a substance or thing. The self-consciousness arises as the existential dependence of one mental state upon another, and so existential dependence—by means of contentual dependence—in general. Now, content dependence, since its origins lie in the givenness of sensation, is thus ultimately dependent upon an external object that for Kant could be the only source of content. Hence the necessary unity of consciousness is made possible by virtue of external objects, the concepts of which (i.e., the concepts of objects, namely the categories) are imposed by us on those contents whose source is derived external to us.

The sceptic, like Hume, claims that there is no meaningful way of referring the contents of consciousness to a numerically identical self.[24] Kant's demonstration *quid juris* answers to sceptical challenge by first agreeing that there is no sense-impression of self, secondly, agreeing that no substantial self can be discovered through introspection, but disagreeing that we cannot thereby refer the contents of consciousness—the representations—to a unity of consciousness. The unity of consciousness reveals itself in the synthetic unity of the manifold, in the contentual interconnection or existential dependence of one mental state upon another. The synthetic unity of the manifold reveals the unity of consciousness as a necessary condition for its possibility. In no other way, in Kant's estimation, can we account for our representations, hence our experience as such.

The empiricists, like Locke, Berkeley, and Hume, encountered great difficulties when they sought to demonstrate the existence of an external world, having begun their investigations by supposing collections of experiences or sense-impressions from which they derived ideas. From Kant's point of view, the approach at demonstration from commonsense belief was doomed to failure; nor did rationalists like Descartes fare any better when they supposed that one could come to grasp self-consciousness by denying the existence of external objects. Kant's critique of Descartes' dogmatic idealism reduces to this: If Descartes was right, he must be wrong; if he was right about the method of doubting, he must be wrong about the self-consciousness that he supposed he discovered after dismissing everything external, since self-consciousness in Kant's view is an activity not a substance. Had he paid more careful attention, Descartes would have discovered, according to Kant, that if he dismissed all external sensations, he would have made self-consciousness impossible.

Kant's objection, more broadly, is directed toward those who suppose that the existence of external objects can at best be inferred. Hume, in the *Treatise* is forced to insist, without argument, that "we must take for granted in all our reasoning" (I, IV, II)[25] the external existence of things like tables and chairs, and Locke before him, in the *Essay* could only assert that the existence of an external world "cannot pass for an ill-grounded confidence" (IV, ix, 3).[26] The demonstration, for Kant, of the existence of the external world proves to be the condition for the possibility of self-consciousness, for without the givenness of external things, self-consciousness would never arise. And, in turn, the self-consciousness that indeed arises is proof, in Kant's estimation, of the "immediate consciousness of the existence of objects outside of me" (B276).

The supposition of the unity of consciousness, as the ultimate condition for the possibility of experience, is both capable of and in need of a proof. But the logic of that demonstration is indeed novel. The ultimate principle—unlike the synthetic a priori principles like causality—is not an object of theoretical knowledge. As in Aristotle's parlance describing an axiom, as that which is necessary for anyone to grasp who is to learn anything at all, so for Kant, the appeal to the unity of consciousness is an appeal to that principle without which it is impossible to grasp anything at all.

In the case of Kant, that principle is not indemonstrable, and it is certainly not obvious, even if its ultimate appeal is to a kind of immediateness. The unobvious unity of consciousness requires a special kind of demonstration in which its immediate status is made apparent. The transcendental argument, thereby, provides a novel strategy to a somewhat novel dilemma, both of which reflect Kant's *Umänderung der Denkart*. Reason discovers, by special demonstration, that it knows without knowing that it knows, that it needs instruction to discover what it has itself put into and imposed upon nature.

In following this argument through the "Refutation of Idealism," we not only provide added support to the claim for Kant's novel employment of the logic of demonstration, but also add the emphasis of Kant's reply to the sceptic who challenges us to show that there is an external world, and challenges us to show how we know. Here Kant argues that the immediacy of self-consciousness is at once the immediacy of the consciousness of external objects.

The argument, and thereby the demonstration of the existence of external objects, first taken up in the fourth "Paralogism" of the A edition is recast in the B edition in the "Analytic" where it properly belongs. This point is effectively made in the B Preface (Bxxxix, x1).[27] The consciousness of my existence is a consciousness in time. As the first analogy has argued, all consciousness in time presupposes something permanent in perception.[28] The permanent cannot be discovered to be within me, by introspection, nor could such a demonstration of an internal and permanent feature of experience be possible. The transcendental deduction has demonstrated that the self is both a transcendental condition and an activity. The self, in terms of the theoretical exegesis of knowledge, is not a substance. The self-consciousness that Kant reveals arises as the contentual dependence of one mental state upon previous mental states that determine it, and so can be distinguished from those representations only by virtue of the necessity in the synthesis. Thus, since the permanent cannot be discovered internally, and since without it experience would be impossible—but, experience is possible because we indeed have it—then there must be a permanent and it must be external to me. Therefore, self-consciousness, which amounts to the awareness of my existence as determined in time, is at once an "immediate consciousness of the existence of other things outside me" (B276).[29]

Epilogue

KANT BELIEVES HIMSELF TO HAVE EFFECTED A REVOLUTION IN PHILOSOPHY on the order of Newton's demonstration of universal gravitation and the general laws of motion, or in terms of Kepler's deduction of the laws of planetary motion. Although he never declares himself to be effecting a Newtonian or Keplerian revolution in philosophy, he explicitly illuminates his efforts in terms of them. To suppose, on the contrary, the commonplace that Kant effects a Copernican—rather than a Newtonian or Keplerian—revolution in philosophy not only commits the trivial error that Kant never makes the claim, but more seriously fosters misunderstanding of the analogy that Kant was indeed drawing when he sought to make clear his contribution to metaphysics on the model of the scientific revolution. To say—as so very many distinguished thinkers have—that Kant effects a Copernican revolution misrepresents Kant's expressed views on the matter, it distorts Kant's view of Copernicus, and it misleads us in our effort to understand what the revolution in science, the very model on which his metaphysics rests, meant to him.

Once we have layed out the structure of the revolution in natural science as Kant envisaged it, we are be in a better position to assess the novelty of his purported revolution in philosophy, and his understanding of developments in scientific knowledge. Kant, struck by the remarkable progress in natural science, came to the conclusion that it was the employment of the hypothetico-deductive method—to use Wolff's parlance—that facilitated its advance. Conscious that metaphysics had fallen into ridicule while natural science became elevated in social esteem, he sought to rectify the deficiencies in rationalist and empiricist metaphysics by adapting the scientific method to philosophical investigations.

The scientific method, as he understood it, offered a concession to the empiricists who demanded that an adequate account of knowledge must take experience seriously: all knowledge, he concluded, indeed begins with experience. But that scientific method, as he adapted it, also offered a concession to the rationalists who demanded that an adequate account of knowledge must ensure certainty: and thus at the same time insisted that all knowledge does not arise from experience—the foundation of knowledge is a priori.

Kant's distortion of that scientific method consisted in his insistence

120

upon the a priori dimension of that procedure. Agreeing with the methodology expressed by Newton in his *Opticks*, Kant sought against Hume, to provide the grounds for a realist interpretation of Newton's physics by exhibiting the most fundamental conditions which underlay the secure path of a science. That argument not only sought to restore the permissibility of causal inference but did so by rejecting a correspondence theory of truth and the similitude theory of reference: by insisting upon the a priori structure of cognition, Kant abandons the commonsense supposition that our mental representations are somehow similar to the objects external to our consciousness which are somehow the source of those mental contents, and thereby rejects the correspondence theory of truth as well. Putnam explores the development of internal realism in terms of just this Kantian change in philosophical agenda, in *Reason, Truth, and History*.

In Kant's estimation, the achievement of *Gewissheit* or "certainty" was secured but it proved to be a curiously relational certainty, as the coherence theory of truth required. The justification of a factual statement consisted in showing the principle that underlay its very possibility, and the principle in turn was shown to be valid insofar as it made intelligible the phenomena by articulating the conditions of that possibility. The certainty Kant secured was too weak for the rationalist programs, and too strong for the programs of the empiricists. But Kant believed the scientific method, as he adapted it to his a priori program, avoided the ridiculous presumptions of the rationalists, and the inescapable scepticism of the empiricists.

When in 1787 Kant characterized his own contribution to metaphysics as a revolution he was drawing inspiration from the American Revolution, by and large (the French Revolution was still two years away). As the practice of revolution, as Kant understood it, sought to emancipate human moral integrity through the founding of a constitution, so Kant envisaged his contribution to be the emancipation of all tiresome and oppressive efforts at exhibiting the limits of human knowledge. The freedom his self-proclaimed revolution secured was the freedom from having to retrace ever again even a single step of the science of human cognition. For he insists that his *Critique* has made all further revolutions both unnecessary and impossible. By imitating the method that he believed secured for natural science *der sichere Gang einer Wissenschaft*, he believed that he had secured for metaphysics that same indisputable royal road.

Kant's project rests on historical arguments that illuminated his path. Those arguments suffer from historical complexities that escaped his notice. He believed it was the discovery of the a priori ingredient in knowing that placed mathematics and natural science on the sure path of science. It seems rather clear that neither the Greek mathematicians, nor the students of nature like Galileo, Torricelli, or Stahl, envisioned their efforts in Kant's terms. These thinkers, despite their differences, were broadly committed to programs that subscribed to transcendental realism—the traditional search for the thing-in-itself—not the empirical realism and transcendental idealism at the heart of Kant's brilliant but brilliantly misguided insight.

But Kant's rendition of the achievement in natural science, despite the dubious historical claims on which his argument rests, became widespread as Kant's first *Critique* grew in importance. A consequence was that insights concerning the nature of science contained in that work became diffused throughout our culture. Kant's project, by his own declarations, rests on an acknowledgement of a scientific revolution that guaranteed certainty. The commonplace in the wide public domain through which his thought has been diffused is that "science is objective, certain, and correct": this is the common, public understanding of the meaning of the so-called scientific revolution. A major objective of this monograph was to unmask the Kantian origins of our contemporary conception of a scientific revolution.

What is unacceptable in Kant's theoretical philosophy is the very same problem that infects our understanding of science in current debates: there is, contrary to Kant's belief, no privileged point of view from which we could declare science to be certain, objective, and ultimately correct. To break through this facade of a scientific revolution is, in part, to abandon the ideology of a privileged context or God's eye point of view. Kant led the way to it, but fell short. He rightly directed us to abandon a search for the thing-in-itself, and thus to see the hopelessness of pursuing external or transcendental realism. But, the internal realism he embraced, because of his insistence upon certainty, retained a commitment to a privileged point of view, this time from the subjective standpoint of cognition. With this unfortunate legacy revealed, the constructive task of securing a meaningful sense of objectivity—while rejecting a privileged point of view in either the object or subject—is the project that lies before us in the metaphysics, epistemology, and the history and philosophy of science. The search for an adequate internal realism seems to offer the greatest promise.

Recent contributions to the history of science have cast into doubt the very idea that a scientific revolution took place—that the sudden, radical, and progressive change that the term "revolution" currently connotes is inappropriate to characterize the historical enterprises that it is designed to illuminate. The ideology of a Copernican revolution, which has become a commonplace, has been, I believe, successfully undermined by Robert Westman and I. Bernard Cohen, among others. Copernicus' contemporaries, with the exception of the impassioned disciple Rheticus, never regarded *De Revolutionibus* as radical in the required sense; further, it took seventy-three years from its publication in 1543 until it appeared in the Catholic Index of Prohibited Books, and almost a century until Galileo was brought to trial for "teaching, holding, and defending" the Copernican theory. The historical circumstances fail to encourage us to see *De Revolutionibus* as analogous to the insurgency at Lexington and Concord, or to the storming of the Bastille, the cases in America or France where "revolution" seems so illuminating. The usefulness of applying the label "Copernican revolution" to Kant's achievement has thus been comparably challenged, over and above the argument that indeed Kant never makes such a Copernican claim. The motivation to think of Kant's effect in terms of a Copernican revolution deserves to be abandoned.

Having cleared away this misguided Copernican path sufficiently to see that we were headed down a dead end, the Wolffian road suggested itself as a more promising path to understand Kant's view of the scientific revolution on whose model he fashioned his metaphysics. Kant learned, or minimally confirmed, his understanding of Copernicus from Wolff, who believed that the progress of science was a consequence of its employment of the hypothetico-deductive method, and who suggested that comparable progress could be made in other enterprises, including philosophy, by imitating that procedure. In the B Preface, Kant announces his plan to imitate the procedure by virtue of which natural science found its way by a sudden and single transformation to the secure road of a science (Bxvi). Copernicus represented for Kant, as he did for Wolff, the proponent of a novel hypothesis, an ingredient in scientific method and progress as indispensable as it was troubling. It was this peculiar sense of hypothesis that escaped the notice of Robert Butts' important ground-breaking studies of Kant's use of hypotheses more than a quarter-century ago. In order to avoid the infelicitous circumstance into which metaphysics, queen of the sciences, had fallen by advancing wild and ridiculous hypotheses, Kant followed Wolff's exhortations admonishing natural science to proceed with all due caution. Wolff insisted that scientists should not publicly declare—should abstain from publishing—their hypotheses until definitively proven, otherwise ridicule and distrust will naturally ensue.

Kant accepts this same tenuous commitment to hypotheses. He agrees with Wolff that hypotheses are indispensable to scientific progress, and that without the definitive proof—the rigorous deduction—they are not to be countenanced especially in the *Critique*. The only reason, therefore, that Kant even mentions Copernicus is that Newton (or Kepler) provides the rigorous deduction which justifies the countenancing of Copernicus' novel hypothesis. This is the most formidable reason why describing Kant's contribution as a Copernican revolution misrepresents his words, misunderstands his thought, and entirely misleads us in our understanding of what the scientific revolution meant to him. To object to speaking of Kant's Copernican revolution is no mere verbal quibble; the objection points to a serious defect in understanding Kant's project.

When he sets out his program in the B Preface in 1787, the analogy with Copernicus is intended to illuminate his novel hypothesis, which he believes he had already proven apodeictically in 1781. In full agreement with Wolff's recommended restraint, the definitive demonstration makes it not merely permissible but desirable to countenance those particular hypotheses that led to great discovery, but only after they have been secured by rigorous deduction. Thus, he publicly announces his hypothesis on the order of the successful hypothesis of Copernicus, but only in the demonstrative light of the *Critique* itself. The positive and indispensable function of hypotheses is thus protected and highlighted. Kant's novel hypothesis, on analogy with Copernicus, is the proposal of a theory of knowledge whose principles were both synthetic and a priori. No sooner does he announce that analogy with Copernicus than he insists that the claim, although merely hypothetical, will be proven apodeictically in the *Critique* itself, as is required by the scientific method he embraced.

The scientific method is adapted in the proof that Kant regards as absolutely—apodeicitically—certain. It consists in a metaphysical deduction that announces the results of Newton's method of analysis or induction—an exhaustive statement of the (unschematized) principles of all certain knowledge; and a transcendental deduction that, following Newton's method of synthesis or deduction, demonstrates the validity of the principles by exhibiting their adequacy to possible experience.

The transcendental deduction is the result of Kant's adaptation of the rigorous deduction demanded by the scientific method to metaphysical pursuits. It follows from his rejection of a correspondence theory of truth and the similitude theory of reference bound up with it. The transcendental deduction displays Kant's commitment to a coherence theory that forced the reinterpretation of the traditional meaning of deduction by showing that certainty was relational not absolute, and that validity consisted in demonstrating that relatedness or applicability of a principle to experience. Through analogy with the scientific method, as he understood it, as stated by Newton in the *Opticks* and reformulated by Wolff in the "Commentationem de Studio Matheseos Recte Instituendo," the idea of demonstration is radically transformed in metaphysics. Rigorous deduction now claims to be justified in two directions: an inference from the premises to a conclusion, as traditionally accepted; and now by analogy with the sciences, an inference from the conclusion (observations/phenomena) back to the premises (causes/principles)—which Wallace in his recent work on Galileo has called the formulation of the "double regressus" argument. It is this sort of revolution that Kant seems to have believed that he effected, on the order of Newton's demonstration. This adaptation and employment of a two directional deduction—a method in sharp contrast with the one directional deduction expounded by Aristotle in the *Posterior Analytics*—is Kant's *Newtonian revolution* in philosophy. If anything deserves to be called revolutionary in Kant's *Critique of Pure Reason*, as triggering a sudden and radical change in the agenda of philosophical programs, it is, I believe, just this.

NOTES

NOTES

Chapter 1.   Introduction

1. I would like to express thanks to the National Endowment for the Humanities for a research grant during the summer of 1985 that made it possible to undertake this project. Special thanks are due to Professor Robert S. Westman, Department of History, at the University of California at Los Angeles, who served as seminar director of the project entitled "Re-Appraisals of 'The Scientific Revolution'." Westman's thoughtfulness forced me to rethink some views that had become well entrenched in my psyche, and I am grateful to be free from some of those inadequate perspectives. Special thanks are also due to my colleague Professor Mark Johnson, who co-taught with me a graduate seminar on Kant's *Critique of Pure Reason* at Southern Illinois University in the autumn of 1985. Johnson has a unique thoughtful ability to provoke me to discover ideas that I never knew were in me. Recognition is also in order for several of my NEH seminar colleagues who were kind enough to read earlier versions of this monograph and comment upon it—Bonnie Paller, Larry Shields, Dick George, and Jutta Birmle. Any faults in this work, however, are mine alone.

2. According to the auction list of Kant's library in 1804, which Arthur Warda discovered and published in 1922, *Immanuel Kants Bücher: Bibliographien und Studien*, Vol. 3, ed. M. Breslauer (Berlin: M. Breslauer, 1922), p. 35, Kant owned a 1719 edition of Newton's *Opticks*.

3. Isaac Newton,*Opticks*, London, 1717 (Great Books of the Western World Series, Encyclopaedia Britannica, Inc., 1948), vol.34, query 31, p. 543.

4. ibid.

5. Cf. Robert S. Hartman, "Kant's Science of Metaphysics and the Scientific Method," *Kant-Studien* 63(1972), pp. 18–35.

6. Hillary Putnam, *Reason, Truth, and History* (Cambridge: At the Univ. Press, 1981), pp. 60–64, esp. p. 64

7. ibid.

8. Thomas Kuhn, *The Structure of Scientific Revolutions* (henceforth *SSR*) (Chicago: Univ. of Chicago Press, 1962, rev. ed. 1970). An important and constructive critical reply can be found in *Paradigms and Revolutions*, ed. G. Gutting (Notre Dame, Ind.: Univ. of Notre Dame Press, 1980), as well as the larger collection in *The Structure of Scientific Theories*, ed. F. Suppe (Urbana: Univ. of Ill. Press, 1977). The reader may wish to consult a succinct summary of the "paradigm" as a "change of world view" in *SSR*, ch. 10, "Revolutions as a Change of World View," pp. 111–135, esp. p. 111, the opening paragraph.

9. Putnam, *Reason, Truth, and History*, pp. 150, 126.

10. Immanuel Kant, *The Critique of Pure Reason*, trans. N. Kemp Smith (1926; New York: St. Martin's Press, 1965 [first published, edition, 1781; revised B edition, 1787]). Kemp Smith translates *mit den ersten Gedanken des Kopernikus* "on the lines of Copernicus' primary hypothesis." This sense seems right, as I shall go on to show, but "with the first thoughts of Copernicus" seems more to the letter of Kant's expression. Unless otherwise noted, all translations from Kant's first *Critique* (henceforth, *KRV*) will be from Kemp Smith.

11. A useful summary and critique of this cumulative dimension of science on Kuhn's assessment can be found in *Progress and its Problems*, by Larry Laudan (Berkeley: Univ. of Calif. Press, 1977).

12. A. Rupert Hall, *The Scientific Revolution: 1500–1800* (London: Longmans, Green, 1954). There is no special reason to single out Hall. The literature in the history of science in the last forty years employs "The Scientific Revolution" as a commonplace.

13. The expressions "scientific revolution" and "Copernicus" have been brought to-

gether many times in literature during this last century, as I show in ch. 4, especially with regard to Kant. The expression "Copernican revolution" has become more popular since Thomas Kuhn's *The Copernican Revolution* (henceforth *CR*) (Cambridge: Harvard Univ. Press, 1957). "The story of the Copernican Revolution has been told many times before. . . ." (Preface, p. 1, first sentence); "The Copernican Revolution was a revolution in ideas. . . ." (Preface, p. 1, first sentence).

14. These facts are well known, but the reader may wish to consult R. S. Westman's "The Copernicans and the Churches," ch. 3, in *God and Nature: The Encounter of Christianity and Science*, ed. D. Lindber and R. Numbers (Berkeley: Univ. of Calif. Press, 1987).

15. Kuhn, *SSR*, discussion of "progress," pp. 160–173, esp. pp. 170–173.

16. W. Stegmuller, "Towards a Rational Reconstruction of Kant's Metaphysics of Experience (I)," *Ratio* (1967), pp. 1–32; and "(II)," *Ratio* (1968), pp. 1–37.

17. G. Buchdahl, "Gravity and Intelligibility: Newton to Kant," in *The Methodological Heritage of Newton*, ed. R. E. Butts and J. W. Davis (Toronto: Univ. of Toronto Press, 1970).

18. G. Brittan, Jr., *Kant's Theory of Science* (Princeton: Princeton Univ. Press, 1978), esp. pp. 117–42.

19. Cf. Robert Paul Wolff, *Kant's Theory of Mental Activity* (Cambridge: Harvard Univ. Press, 1963), for a succinct statement of Hume's challenge to Kant, with regard to the problem of causal inference, p. 25.

20. P. F. Strawson, *The Bounds of Sense* (London: Methuen, 1966). Strawson emphasizes what he calls Kant's "Principle of Significance": "This is the principle that there can be no legitimate or even meaningful, employment of ideas or concepts which does not relate them to empirical or experiential conditions of their application" (p. 16).

21. Ibid. p. 22, "[Kant] believed without question in the finality of Euclidean geometry, Newtonian physics, and Aristotelian logic. . . . "

Chapter 2. Kant's Use of the Term "Revolution"

1. I. Bernard Cohen, *Revolution in Science* (Cambridge: Harvard Univ. Press, Belknap Press, 1985), pp. 237–53, esp. p. 244.

2. Lewis White Beck, "Kant and the Right of Revolution," *Journal of the History of Ideas* 32, 3 (July–Sept. 1971), pp. 411–22.

3. ibid., p. 422.

4. Sidney Axinn, "Kant, Authority, and the French Revolution," *Journal of the History of Ideas* 32, 3 (July–Sept. 1971), pp. 423–32, esp. pp. 431–32.

5. John E. Atwell, "A Brief Commentary" (on Kant on Revolution), *Journal of the History of Ideas* 32, 3 (July–Sept. 1971), pp. 433–36, esp. p. 435.

6. C. Dyke, "Comments" (on Kant on Revolution), *Journal of the History of Ideas* 32, 3 (July–Sept. 1971), pp. 437–40, esp. p. 440.

7. *Immanuel Kant. Sein Leben in Darstellungen von Zeitgenossen/Die Biographien von L. E. Borowski, R. B. Jachmann und A. Ch. Wasianski* (Berlin: Felix Gross, 1912). Cf. Jachmann, sections 77–82, who makes the conversation refer to the American Revolution. But cf. J. H. W. Stuckenberg, *The Life of Immanuel Kant* (London: Macmillan, 1882), who points out, pp. 459–60, n. 88, that something is mistaken in Jachmann's account. For as early as 1770 Hamann dedicated a translation to Green, speaking of him as "the friend of our Kant" (Friedrich Wilhelm Schubert, *Immanuel Kant's Biographie* [Leipzig: Leopold Voss, 1842], p. 53). Thus, Kant and Green could not have met, in 1770 or earlier, while discussing the American Revolution of 1776.

8. H. Heine, *Sämtliche Werke*, ed. Ernest Elster (Leipzig and Vienna: Bibliographisches Institut, 1898), vol. 4, p. 245.

9. Karl Marx/Friedrich Engels, *Historisch-Kritische Gesamtausgabe* (Frankfurt: Marx-Engels-Archiv, 1927), vol. 1, p. 254. Cf. also W. Kegels, "Kant, Marx en de Franse Revolutie," *Dialoog* 10 (1969/70), pp. 78–100; and Karl Vorländer, *Kant und Marx: Ein Beitrag zur Philosophie des Sozialismus* (Tubingen: Mohr, 1911).

10. Cf. A. Zweig, *Kant: Philosophical Correspondences*, 1759–99 (Chicago: Univ. of Chicago Press, 1967), pp. 208–9.

11. I. Kant, "On the Common Saying: 'This May be True in Theory, But It Does Not Apply in Practice'." The German title is "*Über den Gemeinspruch: 'Das mag in der theorie richtig sein, taugt aber nicht fur die Praxis'*," AA 8, pp. 273–313. First published in the *Berlinische Monatsschrift*, 32 (Sept. 1793), pp. 201–84. The English translation is in *Kant's Political Writings*, ed. Hans Reiss, trans. H. B. Nisbet (henceforth, *KPW*/Reiss) (Cambridge: At the Univ. Press, 1970), p. 81.

12. *Allgemeiner Kantindex zu Kants gesammelten Schriften*, vol. 17, ed. Gottfried Martin (Berlin: Walter de Gruyter, 1967), p. 763.

13. I. Kant, "Idea for a Universal History with a Cosomopolitan Purpose," AA 8, pp. 15–31. First published in the *Berlinische Monatsschrift* 4, Nov. 11, 1784, pp. 385–411.

14. Kant, "Idea for a Universal History," in *KPW*/Reiss, p. 48.

15. Ibid., p. 51

16. I. Kant, "What is Enlightenment?" AA 8, pp. 33–42. First published in the *Berlinische Monatsschrift* 4, Dec. 12, 1784, pp. 481–94.

17. Kant, "What is Enlightenment?" in *KPW*/Reiss, p. 55.

18. *Allgemeiner Kantindex*, ed. Gottfried Martin, p. 763.

19. I. Kant, *Religion Within the Limits of Reason Alone*, trans. T. Greene and H. Hudson (1934; New York: Harper, Torchbooks, 1960).

20. Ibid., p. 112.

21. Ibid., pp. 112–13.

22. Ibid., p. 118.

23. Ibid., p. 120.

24. *KPW*/Reiss, p. 82.

25. Ibid.

26. Ibid.

27. Ibid.

28. I. Kant, "Perpetual Peace," AA 8, pp. 341–86. First published in Königsberg by Friedrich Nicolovius, 1795; 2nd enlarged edition, 1796.

29. *KPW*/Reiss, p. 101.

30. *KPW*/Reiss, p. 118.

31. I. Kant, *Metaphysics of Morals*, AA 6, pp. 203–493. First published in Königsberg by Friedrich Nicolovius, 1797.

32. Ibid. *KPW*/Reiss, p. 145 note.

33. Ibid., p. 146

34. Ibid., p. 147

35. Beck, "Kant on the Right of Revolution," p. 417.

36. *KPW*/Reiss, p. 162.

37. Ibid., p. 175

38. Ibid.

39. I. Kant, "Contest of the Faculties," AA 7, pp. 1–116. First published in Königsberg by Friedrich Nicolovius, 1798.

40. *KPW*/Reiss, p. 182

41. Ibid., p. 183.

42. Johann Benjamin Erhard, "Über das Recht des Volkes zu einer Revolution" (Jena, 1794). Erhard (1766–1827), a physician and friend of Kant's published several political treatises. This is the one to which Kant is alluding in "Contest of the Faculties."

43. *KPW*/Reiss, p. 184.

44. Ibid., p. 185.

Chapter 3. Experiment and the Revolution in Science According to the B Preface of 1787

1. Stuckenberg, *Life of Kant*, p. 140. Cf. also Stanley L. Jaki, *Universal Natural History and the Theory of the Heavens* (Edinburgh: Scottish Academic Press, 1981), p. 41.

2. Cf. my discussion of the origins of early Greek science, "What did Thales Want to be When he Grew-Up? or, re-Appraising the Roles of Engineering and Technology on the Origins of Early Greek Science/Philosophy" in *Plato, Time, and Education: Essays in Honor of Robert S. Brumbaugh*, ed. Brian Hendley (Albany: SUNY Albany Press, 1987).

3. Cf. the magisterial work of Walter Burkert, *Lore and Science in Ancient Pythagoreanism*, trans. E. L. Minar Jr. (Cambridge: Harvard Univ. Press, 1972), esp. chs. 4, 5, 6.

4. Stuckenberg, *Life of Kant*, p. 139, referring to the "Hamburger Correspondent," Mar. 7, 1804. Schubert, 141.

5. Stuckenberg, *Life of Kant*, p. 140.

6. Ibid., p. 141. The account was written in 1795.

7. "Als Galilei seine Kugeln die schiefe Fläche mit einer von ihm selbst gewählten Schwere herabrollen. . . ." (Bxii.)

8. Galileo Galilei, *Dialogue Concerning Two Chief World Systems*, trans. Stillman Drake (1632; Berkeley: Univ. of California Press, 1967), from the "First Day," pp. 22–27. According to the catalogue that Warda discovered, Kant owned a 1699 edition of Galileo's *Systema cosmicum*.

9. Galileo Galilei, *Dialogues Concerning Two New Sciences*, trans. H. Crew and A. de Salvio (1914; New York: Dover, 1954), the "Third Day," esp. secs. 205, 218 et seq., pp. 168–169, 184–187.

10. Cristian Wolff, *Elementa Mechanicae* (Halle, 1741); part of the larger work entitled *Elementa Matheseos Universae*, from which Kant taught in 1759 and 1760, discussed below in ch. 6. The *Elementa* is a Latin version, first printed 1713–15, of the German *Die Anfangs-Gründe aller mathematischen Wissenschaften*, first published in 1710. Both versions went through many editions, but later additions were not always included in both versions.

11. Of course, Kant may be thinking of another passage referring to Galileo's efforts, but so far I have not found it.

12. G. Holton, *Foundations of Modern Physical Science* (Reading, Mass.: Addison-Wesley Publishing Co., 1958), pp. 22–33.

13. Alexandre Koyre, "An Experiment in Measurement," *Proceedings of the American Philosophical Society* 97 (1953), pp. 222–37.

14. A. Rupert Hall, "The Significance of Galileo's Thought for the History of Science," in *Galileo: Man of Science*, ed. E. McMullin (N.Y.: Basic Books, 1967), pp. 67–81. " . . . even the positive assertions of experimental verification made by Galileo have been doubted" (p. 73). Cf. also, p. 80, n. 16.

15. Thomas Settle, "An Experiment in the History of Science," *Science* 133 (1961), pp. 19–23; cf. also Settle's "Galileo's use of Experiment as a Tool of Investigation," in *Galileo: Man of Science*, ed. E. McMullin, pp. 315–37. Recently, McLochlin and Drake have published articles adding defense of Settle's claim, arguing that Galileo did indeed undertake the experiment, and that the experiment will provide the required demonstration. Cf. also, Cohen, *Revolution in Science*, p. 404.

16. Norwood Russell Hanson, "Copernicus' Role in Kant's Revolution," *Journal of the History of Ideas* 20 (1959), pp. 274–81, esp. p. 279.

17. Silvio Bedini, "The Instruments of Galileo Galilei," in *Galileo: Man of Science*, ed. E. McMullin pp. 256–92, for a detailed examination of instruments invented or developed by Galileo.

18. Cf. S. Mason, *A History of the Sciences* (New York: Macmillan, Collier Books, 1956), ch. 26, "The Phlogiston theory and the Chemical Revolution," pp. 302–13.

19. Immanuel Kant, *Kritik der reinen Vernunft* (Hamburg: Felix Meiner Verlag, 1956).

The expression *den sicheren Gang einer Wissenschaft* appears for the first time in the second line of the B Preface.

Chapter 4. A Brief Survey of the Secondary Literature on the Expression "Kant's Copernican Revolution"

1. Bertrand Russell, *Human Knowledge: Its Scope and Limits* (London: George Allen & Unwin, 1948), p. 9; John Dewey, *The Quest for Certainty: A Study of the Relation of Knowledge and Action*, Gifford Lectures, 1929 (New York: Minton, Balch & Co., 1929), p. 287; Karl Popper, *Conjectures and Refutations: The Growth of Scientific Knowledge* (New York, London: Basic Books, 1962), p. 180; Ernst Cassirer, *Kant's Life and Thought*, trans. J. Haden, introd., by Stephan Körner (New Haven: Yale Univ. Press, 1981), p. 151, first published in German, in 1918; Karl Jaspers, *Kant*, trans. R. Manheim, ed. Hannah Arendt (New York: Harcourt, Brace & World, 1957), p. 91.

2. When I first wrote this chapter, I. B. Cohen's *Revolution in Science* had not yet been published. I have benefited from reading chapter 15, "Kant's Alleged Copernican Revolution" (pp. 237–54), and discovered some other important thinkers who have propagated the view that Kant effects a Copernican revolution. Cohen's interesting chapter neglects to set Kant's talk of revolution in the first *Critique* in the wider and more ambiguous context of his writings in general.

3. Cf. R. Eisler, *Kant-Lexikon* (Berlin: E. S. Mittler, 1930), which is usually reliable for the first *Critique*, but there is no reference to *dem kopernikanischen Weltsystem* at A 257/B313.

4. S. Körner, in the Introduction to E. Cassirer, *Kant's Life and Thought*, pp. vii–viii.

5. E. Cassirer, *Kant's Life and Thought*, p. 151.

6. Brittan, *Kant's Theory of Science*, pp. 7–12. A central theme of Brittan's work can be thematically described as the antireductionistic thesis. I have made use of his convincing arguments, especially later in the essay.

7. Robert Pippin, *Kant's Theory of Form* (New Haven: Yale Univ. Press, 1982), p. 224, also pp. 8, 232.

8. Roger Scruton, *Kant* (Oxford: At the Univ. Press, Past Masters series, 1982), p. 28.

9. L. W. Beck, "What Have We Learned from Kant?" in *Self and Nature in Kant's Philosophy*, ed. Allen W. Woods (Ithaca, N. Y.: Cornell Univ. Press, 1984), p. 18. Elsewhere, in "Towards a Meta-Critique of Pure Reason," in *Proceedings from the Ottawa Symposium on Kant in the Anglo-American and Continental Traditions*, ed. Pierre Laberge, François Duchesneau, and Bryan Morrissey (Ottawa: Univ. of Ottawa Press, 1976), pp. 182–96, Beck says, on p. 188. "This is the Copernican Revolution in philosophy—the substitution of epistemic for ontological concepts and principles."

10. Gilles Deleuze, *Kant's Critical Philosophy: The Doctrine of the Faculties*, trans. H. Tomlinson and B. Habberjam (Minneapolis: Univ. of Minnesota Press, 1984 [first published in 1963 as *La Philosophie critique de Kant* by Presses Universitaires de France]), pp. 13–14.

11. Strawson, *The Bounds of Sense*, pp. 23, 43–44, 243, 271.

12. T. E. Wilkerson, *Kant's "Critique of Pure Reason"* (Oxford: Clarendon Press, 1967), p. 185.

13. C. D. Broad, *Kant: An Introduction* (Cambridge: At the Univ. Press, 1978), p. 12.

14. Arthur Melnick, *Kant's Analogies of Experience* (Chicago: Univ. of Chicago Press, 1973), p. 152.

15. T. H. Green, *Prolegomena to Ethics*, bk. 1, ch. 1, sec. 11 (first published 1883, reprinted Oxford Univ. Press, 1929). The reader will find a similar but less articulate claim in Victor Cousin, *The Philosophy of Kant* (London: J. Chapman, 1854), p. 21.

16. J. H. Sterling, *Text-book to Kant* (Edinburgh: Oliver and Boyd, 1881), p. 29
17. F. Lange, *History of Materialism*, trans. E. E. Thomas (London: Routledge and Kegan Paul, 1925); vol. 2, pp. 156, 158, 237.
18. Harald Hoffding, *Geschichte der neueren Philosophie* (Leipzig: O. R. Reisland, 1896), vol. 2, p. 64. (Trans. B. E. Meyer, *A History of Modern Philosophy*, [New York: Humanities Press, 1950]).
19. Samuel Alexander, *Hibbert Journal*, Oct. 1909, p. 49.
20. Russell, *Human Knowledge*, p. 9.
21. Norman Kemp Smith, *A Commentary to Kant's "Critique of Pure Reason"* (1918; New York: Humanities Press, 1962), pp. 22–25.
22. J. Watson, *The Philosophy of Kant Explained* (Glasgow: James Maclehose and Sons, 1908), p. 37.
23. This proves to be T. Weldon's position in his *Introduction to Kant's "Critique of Pure Reason"* (Oxford: Clarendon Press, 1945), p. 77, note.
24. Kemp Smith, *Commentary to Kant's "Critique of Pure Reason,"* p. 25.
25. H. J. Paton, *Kant's Metaphysic of Experience*, 2 vols. (New York: Macmillan, 1936), vol. 1, p. 75.
26. A. C. Ewing, *A Short Commentary on Kant's Critique of Pure Reason* (Chicago: Univ. of Chicago Press, 1938), p. 16.
27. C. J. Friedrich, *The Philosophy of Kant* (New York: Random House, Modern Library, 1949), p. xxvii.
28. Hanson, "Copernicus' Role in Kant's Revolution."
29. S. Morris Engel, "Kant's Copernican Analogy: A Re-examination," *Kant-Studien* 54 (1963), pp. 243–51.
30. J. N. Findlay, *Kant and the Transcendental Object: A Hermeneutic Study* (Oxford: At the Univ. Press, 1981), p. 128.
31. Karl Ameriks, *Kant's Theory of Mind: An Analysis of the Paralogisms of Pure Reason* (Oxford: Clarendon Press; New York: Oxford Univ. Press, 1982), pp. 5–8.
32. T. K. Swing, *Kant's Transcendental Logic* (New Haven: Yale Univ. Press, 1969), p. 358.
33. I. Kant, [*Contest of the Faculties*], *On History*, trans. and ed. L. W. Beck (New York: Bobbs-Merrill, 1958), pp. 141–42.

Chapter 5. Kant's Revolution
and the Ambiguous Use of Hypotheses

1. Kemp Smith, *Commentary on Kant's "Critique of Pure Reason,"* p. xx.
2. Robert E. Butts, "Hypothesis and Explanation of Kant's Philosophy of Science," *Archiv fur Geschichte der Philosophie* 43 (1961), pp. 153–70.
3. Robert E. Butts, "Kant on Hypotheses in the 'Doctrine on Method' and the *Logic,"* *Archiv fur Geschichte der Philosophie* 44 (1962), pp. 185–204, esp. pp. 187–88.
4. Ibid.
5. Christiano von Wolfio, *Elementa Matheseos Universae*, from the section entitled "Commentationem de Studio Matheseos Recte Instituendo," sec. 310.
6. Quoted by Jaspers, *Kant*, p. 91.

Chapter 6. Kant, Copernicus, and the Copernican Revolution in Philosophy

1. Kemp Smith, *Commentary to Kant's "Critique of Pure Reason,"* p. 24.

2. Three useful sources on Kant's biography and intellectual development: Emil Arnoldt, *Kritische Exkurse im Gebiete der Kantforschung (Gesammelte Schriften,* Bd. 4) 2 vols. (Berlin: B. Cassirer, 1908–11); Hans Dietrich Irmscher, ed., *Immanuel Kant, Aus den Vorlesungen der Jahre 1762 bis 1764. Aus Grund der Nachschriften Johann Gottfried Herders, Kant-Studien* 88 (Cologne, 1964); and most recently, Gottfried Martin, *Arithmetic and Combinatorics: Kant and His Contemporaries,* trans. Judy Wubnig (Carbondale: Southern Ill. Univ. Press, 1985), esp. pp. xx–xxvii, and pp. 142–45.

3. Scruton, *Kant,* p. 3.

4. This is ultimately the same conclusion reached by Hanson, in "Copernicus' Role in Kant's Revolution." And it is a point of view shared by Ted Humphrey, in "Kant's 'Copernican Revolution' and the Certainty of Geometrical Knowledge," in *Reflections on Kant's Philosophy,* ed. W. H. Werkmeister (Gainesville: Univ. Presses of Fla., 1975), pp. 149–75. Humphrey is specifically concerned with how Kant's Copernican revolution squares with a problem concerning metric space.

5. If Copernicus' theory did not offer a more accurate model for prediction, then why did anyone become a Copernican? The answer Kuhn offers is "as Copernicus himself recognized, the real appeal of the sun-centered astronomy was aesthetic rather than pragmatic. To astronomers the initial choice between Copernicus' system and Ptolemy's could only be a matter of taste, and matters of taste are the most difficult of all to define or debate." (*CR,* p. 172.)

6. Cf. Robert S. Westman, "The Copernicans and the Churches," in *God and Nature,* ch. 3, p. 3.

7. Ibid. Cf. also, Kuhn, *CR,* pp. 173, 177–79.

8. Nicolas Copernicus, *[De Revolutionibus], On the Revolutions of the Heavenly Spheres* (Great Books of the Western World series, Encyclodaedia Britannica Inc., 1939), vol. 16, bk. 1, ch. 1, p. 511.

9. Westman, from *God and Nature,* ch. 3, p. 6.

10. Copernicus, *[De Revolutionibus],* bk. 1, ch. 1, p. 511.

11. Ibid, bk. 1, ch. 2, p. 511.

12. Aristotle, *DeCaelo,* II, 14, 297b24–31. Aristotle argues for the sphericity of the earth in chapter 14 of book 2, in which he begins by examining whether or not the earth is in motion. The argument proposed, for the earth's sphericity is that during a lunar eclipse, the moon is always bounded by a convex arc (*aei kupten exei ten horizousin grammen,* 297b29–30). The argument is mathematically inconclusive, independent of the difficulty of establishing the precise curve observed. Cf. O. Neugebauer's *A History of Ancient Mathematical Astronomy,* 3 vols. (Berlin and New York: Springer-Verlag, 1975), pt. 3, pp. 1093–94: "But even if we take it for granted that the shadow of some object on another unknown surface appears as a circle one should remember that there exists an unlimited number of shadow casting and shadow receiving bodies which produce identical shadow limits. Furthermore, assuming the sphericity of the earth, moon, and sun the shadow curve on the moon is the intersection of a circular cone with a sphere, thus an algebraic space curve of the fourth order and part of its projection on the celestial sphere is what we see as the boundary of the shadow."

13. Copernicus, *[De Revolutionibus],* bk. 1, ch. 2, pp. 511–12.

14. Ibid., bk. 1, ch. 5 ("Does the Earth Have a Circular Movement? And of its Place"), pp. 514–15.

15. A. Birkenmajer, "Comment Copernic a-t-il conçu et réalisé son oeuvre?" In *Organon,* 1936, reprinted in *Etudes d'histoire des sciences en Pologne, Studia Copernicana* 4 (Warsaw: Ossolineum, 1972), pp. 589–611. For notes 153–58, cf. Introduction, *The Copernican Achievement,* ed. R. S. Westman (Berkeley: Univ. of Calif. Press, 1975), p. 3.

16. Noel Swerdlow, "The Derivation and First Draft of Copernicus' Planetary Theory: A Translation of the *Commentariolus* with Commentary," *Proceedings of the American Philosophical Society* (1973), vol. 117, pp. 471–76.

17. J. L. E. Dreyer, *A History of Astronomy from Thales to Kepler*, 2nd ed. (New York: Dover Books, 1953), pp. 310–16.

18. This position has had adherents, like Edward Rosen, in *Three Copernican Treatises* (New York: Columbia Univ. Press, 1939), Introduction, p. viii.

19. J. E. Ravetz, *Astronomy and Cosmology in the Achievement of Nicolas Copernicus* (Warsaw: Zakxad Narodowy im. Ossolińskich, 1965); also "The Origins of the Copernican Revolution," in *Scientific American* 215, no. 4 (Oct. 1966), pp. 88–98.

20. Curtis Wilson, "Rheticus, Ravetz, and the 'Necessity' of Copernicus' Innovation," in *The Copernican Achievement*, ed. R. S. Westman (Berkeley: Univ. of Calif. Press, 1975), p. 17–39.

21. Hanson, "Copernicus' Role in Kant's Revolution," p. 276.

22. Ibid., 277.

23. Erich Adickes, *Kant als Naturforscher*, 2 vols. (Berlin, 1924–25), vol. 1, p. 11n.

24. Cassirer, *Kant's Life and Thought*, p. 42.

25. Hanson, "Copernicus' Role in Kant's Revolution," p. 280.

26. Ibid., p. 277 and n. 11. Two other studies, particularly on Kant's Copernican revolution are worthy of mention. In 1963, S. Engel investigated the Copernican analogy, in "Kant's Copernican Analogy: A Re-Examination," in *Kant-Studien* 54 (1963), pp. 243–51, though he does not seem to be aware of Hanson's article. In 1964, Olivier replied briefly and caustically to Engel's article, in a short essay entitled "Kant's Copernican Analogy: An Examination of a Re-Examination," in *Kant-Studien* 55 (1964), pp. 505–11.

27. Kant's 1759 letter to Lindner, in Cassirer, *Kant's Life and Thought*, p. 42.

28. Wolff, *Elementa Matheseos Universae* (1741 edition), vol. 5, pp. 169–526; esp. ch. 9, "De Studio Astronomie," pp. 450–99. Cf. also, Cassirer, *Kant's Life and Thought*, p. 42, n. 9, which discusses Kant's teaching schedule. The announcement concerning classes that Kant was supposed to teach at that time comprise thirty-four to thirty-six hours per week. It is not clear that and how he could have carried out this program.

29. All the citations from Wolff are taken from the 1746 text "Commentationem de Studio Matheseos Recte Instituendo," published in Geneva—following Hanson/Adickes—which Kant supposedly used. I have checked the relevant passages against the 1741 edition of the *Elementa Mechanicae*, specifically the *"Commentationem de Studio Matheseos Recte Instituendo"* in Hallae. All the citations I have encountered, in the relevant passages, have been identical.

30. Thus, Wolff insists upon the use of hypotheses but expresses grave concern about premature publication, since the publication of hypotheses masquerading as serious claims can only undermine confidence in an otherwise sound practice. In the A Preface, Kant's refusal to deal in hypotheses is emphasized in the name of a demand for *Gewissheit*. Despite the claim in the General Scholium of Newton's *Principia* that "I feign no hypotheses . . .", Wolff attends to just this matter, in section 309. Newton does not eliminate hypotheses; Wolff corrects the misapprehension by insisting that he makes use of them himself. But there are those who think Newton meant to abstain from any hypotheses, and advise others to do so as well. *"Diximus non-nulla huc spectantia in Discursu praeliminari de Philosophia, quem Logicae praemisimus, methodum philosophicam explicantes. Laudant quidam Newtonum, quod ex Philosophia naturali eliminaverit hypotheses; qui tamen hypothesibus indulget in iis ipsis, in quibus eum ab iifdem abstinuisse existimant."*

31. The likely fact that Kant never read Copernicus' *De Revolutionibus* should not strike us as entirely surprising. Newton evidently learned his Kepler from Thomas Streete's *Astronomia Carolina*, 1661, that is, secondhand, as discussed by D. T. Whiteside. (See, e.g.: "Patterns of Mathematical Thought in the Later Seventeenth Century," *Archive for History of Exact Sciences* 1 [1960–62], pp. 179–338; "Expanding World of Newtonian Research," *History of Science* 1 [1962], pp. 16–29, 86–90, 96–100; "Newton's Marvellous Year 1666 and All That," *Notes and Records of the Royal Society of London*

20 [1966], pp. 32–41; "Before the *Principia*: The Maturing of Newton's Thoughts on Dynamical Astronomy, 1664–1684," *Journal for the History of Astronomy* 1 [1970], pp. 5–19; "The Mathematical Principles Underlying Newton's *Principia Mathematica*," *Journal for the History of Astronomy* 1 [1970], pp. 116–38.) I am supposing that Kant learned his Copernicus in a comparable fashion from Wolff, and this would mean that Kant is in dialogue with Wolff, in which Copernicus is the subtext.

Chapter 7. Rethinking the Revolutionary Contributions of Copernicus and Galileo to the Natural Science That Kant Understood

1. Cohen, *Revolution in Science*, pp. 123–25, esp. p. 125.
2. Kuhn, *CR*, p. 1.
3. According to the catalogue that Warda discovered listing Kant's books auctioned in 1808, evidently Kant owned a 1699 edition of Galileo's *Dialogue* under the title *Systema cosmicum*.
4. Wolff, *Elementa* (1741), vol. 5, cf. the "Index Autorum," at the close of the treatise on scientific method. The pages are not numbered but the references can be located under "G."
5. Galileo, *Dialogues*, p. 453.
6. Ibid., pp. 453, 454; and it is worth noting that changes in tides corresponding to solstices and equinocti had been associated with the sun, prior to Galileo. Cf. *Galileo: Man of Science*, ed. E. McMullin, p. 41.
7. Wolff, *Elementa* (1741), vol. 5, pp. 5–164.
8. Wolff, *Elementa* "Commentationem de Praecipuis Scriptis Mathematicis," vol. 5, p. 109.
9. Ibid., p. 108.
10. Wolff, *Die Anfangs-Gründe* (1750 edition), which Kant owned, vol. 4, pp. 132–33.
11. Wolff, *Elementa* (1741), vol. 5, p. 484.
12. Ibid., p. 485.
13. This is effectively the procedure Newton follows in the *Principia*. In book 1, section 3, Newton provides in propositions 11 and 12 (also in proposition 10, in section 2) an investigation of the motion of bodies in eccentric conic sections. In section 12, proposition 71, Newton sets out the inverse square law operating upon bodies moving in elliptical orbits. Cf. Isaac Newton's *Mathematical Principles of Natural Philosophy* (first published 1687), Andrew Motte's 1729 translation, revised with commentary by Florian Cajori (Berkeley: Univ. of Calif. Press, 1934).
14. *The Copernican Achievement*, ed. R. S. Westman (*God and Nature*), ch. 3 p. 3.
15. For an illuminating discussion of the hierarchy of the sciences in Aristotle, cf. Joseph Owens, *Aristotle: The Collected Papers of Joseph Owens*, ed J. Catan (Albany: State Univ. of N. Y. Press, 1981), "The Aristotelian Conception of the Sciences," pp. 23–35. Cf. also Joseph Marietan, *Problème de la classification des sciences d'Aristote à St. Thomas* (Paris: F. Alcan, 1901), and Robert McRae, *The Problem of the Unity of the Sciences: Bacon to Kant* (Toronto: Univ. of Toronto Press, 1961), esp. p. vii.
16. Ptolemy, *Almagest*, trans. R. Catesby Taliaferro (Great Books Series, Encyclopedia Britannica Inc., 1939). In the very opening sentence of book 1, Ptolemy says that "Those who have been true philosphers . . .seem to me to have wisely separated the theoretical part of philosophy from the practical" (p. 5). And this is the basic division that he shall pursue in the astronomy, separating the theoretical or mathematical part from the practical or physical.
17. Apparent irregularities in planetary motion, accounting for changes of brightness

and speed, are discussed in the *Almagest*, book 9, chapter 2, "On the Aim of Planetary Hypotheses."

18. The insistence upon regular and circular motions is maintained throughout, cf. *Almagest*, p. 270; this sentiment is repeated elsewhere, and is supposed in the very idea of Ptolemy's calculations. In *Almagest*, book 3, chapter 3, "On the Hypotheses Concerning Regular and Circular Movement," Ptolemy prefaces his remarks about apparent irregularities in the movement of the sun by insisting that "it is first necessary to assume in general that the motions of the planets . . .are all regular and circular by nature" (p. 86).

19. *The Copernican Achievement*, ed. R. S. Westman (*God and Nature*), ch. 3, p. 2.

20. Ibid.

21. Cf. James A. Weisheipl, "Classification of the Sciences in Medieval Thought," *Medieval Studies* 27 (1965), pp. 50–90, esp. pp. 82–84.

22. Pierre Gassendi, *Institutio astronomica* (1647), which Kant owned, and was included in Warda's library list. And Gassendi, no doubt, learned of Osiander's letter from Kepler's work in 1609.

23. Hanson, "Copernicus' Role in Kant's Revolution," p. 277–13. "Professor Kemp Smith mistakenly refers to the Osiander portion in the name of Copernicus, in order to show how the latter regarded his 'hypothesis.' "

24. Copernicus, [*De Revolutionibus*], p. 506.

25. A demonstration is more than a deduction (*sullogismos*); Aristotle in his *Posterior Analytics*, admits that there can be a deduction without a demonstration (*apodeixis*) [71b22–25].

26. Sir David Ross, *Aristotle's Prior and Posterior Analytics* (Oxford: At the Univ. Press, 1949), pp. vii, xxi.

27. Jonathan Barnes, "Aristotle's Theory of Demonstration," in *Articles on Aristotle*, vol. 1, ed. J. Barnes, M. Schofield, R. Sorabji, (London: Duckworth, 1975), pp. 65–87, esp. pp. 77 and 85.

28. W. K. C. Guthrie, *A History of Greek Philosophy*, vol. 6, *Aristotle: An Encounter* (Cambridge: At the Univ. Press, 1981), pp. 170–71.

29. A *locus classicus* for the distinction in Aristotle between the *hoti* and *dioti* argument appears in the *Posterior Analytics*, chapter 13, 78a23–79a16. In a syllogism, the essence or cause is presented as the middle term. In a demonstrative syllogism, a demonstration of the reasoned fact *dioti*, the actual or true cause is presented, which explains the reason for the conclusion. In a formally similar argument that presents the mere fact (*hoti*), the middle term that purports to be the cause is in fact not the cause of the conclusion. In the first example, 78a32–35, the planets are supposed to be near because they twinkle; the second example corrects this *hoti* case, for the planets twinkle because they are near. The reason why the planets twinkle is because they are near; the isolation of the correct middle term thus distinguishes the mere deduction from the rigorous demonstration.

30. Cf. William A. Wallace, *Galileo and His Sources: The Heritage of the Collegio Romano in Galileo's Science*, (Princeton, N. J.: Princeton Univ. Press, 1984). Galileo's treatment of logical questions are discussed in ch. 1, pp. 3–51.

31. Ibid., p. 123.

32. Cf. E. A. Burtt, *The Metaphysical Foundations of Modern Science* (New York: Humanities Press, 1954), ch. 3, pp. 73–104. Of Galileo, Burtt says, "just consider that the history of thought must turn to a single individual as the one who, by experimental disproof, overthrew a hoary science" (p. 103). Wallace succeeds in showing that Galileo could follow the Aristotelian tradition vis-à-vis the Collegio Romano, rather than the Aristotelians at the Italian universities.

33. Wallace, *Galileo and his Sources*, p. 99.

34. Ibid.

35. Wolff, *Elementa*, sec. 311.

36. The preoccupation, in the "Transcendental Doctrine of Method," in the section on the "Discipline of Pure Reason," makes it clear that mathematics and philosophy proceed in opposing fashions. That discussion begins at A713/B741 and continues effectively

through A720/B748. Kant returns to these distinctions again in the passage at A724/B752 and continues it intermittently throughout the remainder of that section.

37. Cf. Kemp Smith, who in his *Commentary to Kant's "Critique of Pure Reason,"* recognizes this "strangely perverse" situation in which Kant, on the one hand, asserts the secure path of logic and accepts its finality, and, on the other hand, does so "in the act of revolutionizing the traditional logic" (p. 184).

38. Cassirer, *Kant's Life and Thought*, p. 42.

Chapter 8. Kant's Copernican Hypothesis: Science, Metaphysics, and the Pursuit of Synthetic a priori Judgments

1. For an excellent discussion of Kant's legislative model in the *Critique*, cf. Deleuze, *Kant's Critical Philosophy*. The work follows through the legislative metaphor through all three *Critiques*.

2. Precisely what relation inheres between Newton's pronouncement of the laws of motion at the opening of the *Principia* and Kant's *Analogies of Experience*, has been a subject of debate. The issue has been taken up by Buchdahl, Stegmüller, Brittan, Melnick, and others. I follow Brittan's general position, "What follows from what Kant calls the 'unity of consciousness' is not Newtonian physics, or the 'validity' of Newtonian physics, but rather the possibility of providing a realist or material interpretation of Newtonian physics. Kant's great insight in the transcendental deduction is that the unity of consciousness amounts to the possibility of being able to distinguish between what is objective and what is subjective in our experience and that this possibility in turn requires more than a minimal interpretation of Newton's (or any comparable) theory." (*Kant's Theory of Science*, p. 126.)

3. Whether there are eight or twelve a priori principles depends, in part, on how one counts. Since Kant insists that there is a category supposed by each and every one of the logical forms of judgment, and since there are twelve such logical forms articulated, then it would seem that there must indeed be twelve a priori concepts or categories. When they are schematized, however, we are only given eight.

4. This is an important point. In the attempt to demonstrate how natural science can be a science, that is, how synthetic a priori propositions are possible in natural science, Kant at once articulates the foundation of a constructive metaphysics, and to that extent, the science of metaphysics and natural science share the same demonstration.

5. G. W. Leibniz, *Monadology*, in *Leibniz: The Monadology*, trans. R. Latta (Oxford: At the Univ. Press, 1951), secs. 31, 32, 33, esp. 33: "There are also two kinds of truths, those of reasoning and those of fact. Truths of reasoning are necessary and their opposite is impossible: truths of fact are contingent and their opposite is possible." (Pp. 235–36.)

6. David Hume, *Enquiries Concerning the Human Understanding* [1777], ed. L. A. Selby-Bigge, 2nd ed. (Oxford: Clarendon Press, 1902), p. 95; and also section 4, "The contrary of every matter of fact is still possible because it can never imply a contradiction and is conceived by the mind with the same facility and distinctness as if ever so comfortable to reality." So much for the synthetic character of "matters of fact." On the other hand, the analytic character of "relations of ideas" are presented as "discoverable by the mere operation of thought without dependence on what is anywhere existent in the universe."Cf. also, W. A. Suchting, "Hume and Necessary Truth," *Dialogue* (1966–67), pp. 47–60.

7. This issue concerning Locke is interesting because Kant refers to Locke explicitly in the *Prolegomena* where at AA20. 322, Kant supposes Locke to provide "an indication of the division." There, Kant refers us to chapter 3, sections 9–10 of Locke's *Essay*. Why book 4, chapters 7–8, escaped his notice is unclear. For there, Locke distinguishes clearly—

no "mere" indication—of just this difference, calling them "trifling" versus "instructive" propositions.

8. R. Carnap, "Introductory Remarks" to the English edition of Hans Reichenbach's *The Philosophy of Space and Time*, trans. M. Reichenbach and H. Freund (New York: Dover Publications, 1958), pp. vi–viii; R. Carnap, *The Logical Structure of the World* (Berkeley: Univ. of Calif. Press, 1967); and "Empiricism, Semantics and Ontology," Appendix A in R. Carnap, *Meaning and Necessity* (Chicago: Univ. of Chicago Press, 1956).

9. C. I. Lewis, *An Analysis of Knowledge and Valuation* (La Salle, Ill.: Open Court Publishing Co., 1946), esp. ch. 8; and C. I. Lewis, *Mind and the World Order* (New York: Dover Publications, 1956), esp. p. 190n.

10. A. Lovejoy, "Kant's Antithesis of Dogmatism and Criticism," *Mind* (1906), reprinted in M. S. Gram, ed. *Kant: Disputed Questions* (Chicago: Univ. of Chicago Press, 1967), pp. 105–30.

11. L. W. Beck, "Lovejoy as a Critic of Kant," *Journal of the History of Ideas* 30 (1972), pp. 471–84.

12. L. W. Beck, "Analytic and Synthetic Judgments before Kant," in *Reflections on Kant's Philosophy*, ed. W. H. Werkmeister (Gainesville: Univ. Presses of Fla., 1975), pp. 7–27. My analysis has benefited considerably from this second piece by Beck.

13. Kant's letter to K. L. Reinhold, May 12, 1789, in A. Zweig's *Kant: Philosophical Correspondences 1759–99* (Chicago: Univ. of Chicago Press, 1967), p. 141.

14. Ibid.

15. Beck, "Analytic and Synthetic Judgments before Kant," p. 20.

16. Expressed in terms of the inevitable problem of third-man arguments is yet a different way to share Brittan's view of Kant's antireductionistic project, discussed in *Kant's Theory of Science*, esp. ch. 1.

17. Kant, *KRV*, "Obviously there must be some third thing, which is homogeneous on the one hand with the category, and on the other hand with the appearance, and which thus makes the application of the former to the latter possible." (A138/B177.)

18. Beck, "Analytic and Synthetic Judgments before Kant," p. 9.

19. Leibniz argued that the foundation of mathematics is the Principle of Contradiction. In Leibniz' second paper, replying to Clarke, he insists that "This single principle is sufficient to demonstrate every part of arithmetic and geometry, that is, all mathematical principles." *The Leinbiz-Clarke Correspondence*, ed. H. G. Alexander (New York: Philosophical Library, 1956), p. 15. But, Leibniz extended this reductionistic program to all contingent propositions as well; he argued that even contingent propositions can be known a priori. Cf. discussions in G. H. R. Parkinson, *Logic and Reality* in Leibniz's Metaphysics (Oxford; Clarendon Press, 1965), p. 66, and L. W. Beck, *Early German Philosophy* (Cambridge: At the Univ. Press, 1969), pp. 210–11.

20. Certainly this is how Kant saw it; cf. the letter to Reinhold replying to Eberhard's charge (note 13, above).

21. Ralph C. S. Walker, *Kant: The Arguments of the Philosophers* (London: Routledge & Kegan Paul, 1978), pp. 3–5. Walker tries to set the stage with Leibniz' project, critiques by Wolff and Crusius, and Kant's adoption of a modified Crusius-plan.

22. Beck, "Analytic and Synthetic Judgments before Kant," esp. pp. 18–19. Kant does not follow Crusius' constructive plan but recognizes the challenge to distinguish between logical grounds as opposed to real grounds for judgments. Beck eloquently sums up the point: "But what Kant did learn from Crusius must not be underestimated; he learned that 'the rain never follows the wind because of the law of identity.' " (P. 19.)

23. Leibniz, cf. notes 5 and 19, above.

24. Walker, *Kant: The Arguments of the Philosophers*, p. 4.

25. Cf. Brittan, *Kant's Theory of Science*, chapter 1: "The Anti-Reductionist Kant."

26. Walker, *Kant: The Arguments of the Philosophers*, pp. 2–5.

27. Consider the following passages, from Kant, *KRV*, all of which insist that meaning re-

quires the reference to objects, and that requires a given sensible intuition, without which there could be no meaning at all:

> We demand in every concept, first, the logical form of a concept (of thought) in general, and secondly, the possibility of giving it an object to which it may be applied. In the absence of such object, it has no meaning, and is completely lacking in content (A239/B298.)
>
> Therefore, all concepts, and with them all principles, even such as are possible *a priori*, relate to empirical intuitions, that is, to the data of possible experience. Apart from this relation, they have no objective validity. . . .Although all these principles, and the representation of the object with which this science occupies itself, are generated in the mind completely *a priori*, they would mean nothing, were we not always able to present their meaning in appearances, that is, empirical objects. We therefore demand that a bare concept be made sensible, that is, an object corresponding to it be presented in intuition. (A239/B298–A240/B299.)

28. This has not made commentators any happier. For the general criticism of Kant's philosophy of mathematics, a la Carnap and C. I. Lewis (See nn. 8 and 9, above), is that there are no such synthetic a priori propositions in mathematics. The brunt of criticism challenges Kant to show that mathematical propositions are synthetic. His insistence that they are follows the nonreductionistic program.

29. Cf. the discussion in Brittan, *Kant's Theory of Science*, ch. 3, esp. pp. 72–73.

Chapter 9. Kant's Newtonian Revolution: Transcendental Arguments and the Requirement of Demonstration in the *Critique*

1. Körner, in the Introduction to Cassirer, *Kant's Life and Thought*, p. viii, described Kant's Copernican revolution in philosophy to announce two new kinds of questions, one *quid facti* and the other *quid juris*.

2. Kant, *KRV*, "The system of the Principles of the Pure Understanding." "The proposition that no predicate contradictory of a thing can belong to it, is entitled the principle of contradiction, and is a universal, though merely negative, criterion of truth." (Af151/B190.) "The principle of contradiction must therefore be recognized as being the universal and completely sufficient principle of all analytic knowledge." (A151/B191.)

3. This insistence upon requiring that meaning be connected to the capacity of a concept to refer to really possible objects of experience is emphasized in this section of *KRV*, as well as later in summary in the section entitled "Phenomena/Noumena."

> If knowledge is to have objective validity, that is, to relate to an object, and is to acquire meaning and significance in respect to it, the object must be capable of being in some manner given. Otherwise concepts are empty; through them we have indeed thought, but in this thinking we have really known nothing. . . . [Even concepts represented in the mind completely a priori] would yet be without objective validity, senseless and meaningless, if their necessary application to the objects of experience were not established. . . . Apart from these objects of experience, they [i.e., categories] would be devoid of meaning. (A155/B194–A156/B195.)

4. Kant had reached this position as early as the inaugural dissertation of 1770. Cf. an interesting discussion of what is new and what is found in Kant's earlier writings, Walker,

Kant: The Arguments of the Philosophers, chs. 3 and 4, pp. 28–59. Cf. also, Wilkerson, *Kant's "Critique of Pure Reason,"* esp. pp. 36–41.

5. Kant insists in *KRV* that sensibility and understanding must be treated separately. This is part of the antireductionistic strategy. And yet, in a curious comment in the Introduction he leaves open the possibility that there is some more fundamental connection between the two, but that it remains unknown to us. " . . .we need only say that there are two stems of human knowledge, namely, sensibility and understanding, which perhaps spring from a common, but to us unknown, root." (A15/B29.)

6. Among the most hostile critics on this dimension of Kant's project is Wilkerson, *Kant's "Critique of Pure Reason."* "I see no point in paying attention to the Schematism here, save to record its existence. . . . (P. 71.)" . . .the Schematism serves no useful purpose and can in my opinion be ignored without loss." (P. 94.)

7. The treatment of imagination in section 24 of the B Deduction, B151, is rather obscure. I have come to appreciate the difficulty and importance of the role of the imagination as a result of conversations with Professor Mark Johnson, with whom I co-taught a graduate seminar on Kant's *Critique of Pure Reason* in the autumn semester of 1985. In that B151 passage, Kant vacillates between declaring that the imagination belongs to sensibility, and on the other hand, belongs to the understanding. Since Kant has tried to maintain a radical separation between these two faculties, the role of imagination is all the more perplexing.

8. Wilkerson, *Kant's "Critique of Pure Reason,"* rightly criticizes this sort of move as "Kant's attempt to conjure the categories . . ." a move which he accurately describes as disastrous. [p. 46].

9. Kemp Smith, *Commentary to Kant's "Critique of Pure Reason,"* p. 184, calls this move "strangely perverse."

10. Hegel, vol. 5, sec. 52, in the Glochner edition, quoted by Gottfried Martin, *Kant's Metaphysics and Theory of Science*, trans. P. G. Lucas (Manchester: Manchester Univ. Press, 1955), p. 87. Martin agrees that Hegel's assertion is correct. "Kant himself gave no proof of the completeness of the table, and if any such proof is offered, it must always be doubtful whether it really is a Kantian proof." (P. 87.)

11. Martin, *Kant's Metaphysics and Theory of Science.*

12. Cf. Aristotle's *Posterior Analytics*, trans. with notes by J. Barnes (Oxford: Clarendon Press, 1975), pp. 106–7.

13. The text at *Posterior Analytics*, 85b27–28, reads: *hoste hai he apodeixis beltion, mallon gar tou aitiou kai tou dia ti estin*, "Therefore, universal demonstration is better, because it is more properly [a demonstration] of the cause or reasoned fact."

14. So, in the "Postulates of Empirical Thought," in *KRV*, Kant can say of the a priori categories " . . .we obtain confirmation that the categories are not themselves knowledge, but are merely forms of thought for the making of knowledge from given intuitions" (A235/B288). The categories are valid only so far as they are employed in possible experience. The validity of the a priori principles are in just as much need—so far as their validity is concerned—to be shown applicable to possible experience, as possible experience is in need of a demonstration of the conditions of its a priori possibility.

15. Newton, *Opticks*, Query 31; the relevant passage was quoted by me in full at the close of sec. 1.A in ch.1, "Introduction." Cf. ch. 1, nn. 3 and 4.

16. Barry Stroud, "Transcendetal Arguments," reprinted in *The First Critique: Reflections on Kant's Critique of Pure Reason*, ed. T. Penelhum and J. J. MacIntosh (Belmont, Calif.: Wadsworth Publishing Co., 1969), pp. 54–69, esp. p. 65.

17. Ibid. " . . .transcendental arguments are supposed to prove that certain particular concepts are necessary for experience or thought; they establish the necessity or indispensability of certain concepts" (p. 56).

18. Ted Humphrey, in "Kant's 'Copernican Revolution,' " uses the expression "self-motivated thinking activity"—a useful locution—support for which he finds in Kant's "Prize" essay where he uses the word *willkürliche*.

19. Cf. H. W. Cassirer, *Kant's Critique of Pure Reason* (London: Humanities Press, 1968). Cassirer puts it nicely in describing the relation between the unity of consciousness and the unity in objects. "The unity which is to be found in an object consists in being brought before a unitary self. The unity of the self consists in its coming to recognize that unity which is manifested in every object of sense-experience." (P. 75.)

20. I argued just this position in 1977 in "Necessity, Objectivity, and the Structure of Transcendental Arguments in the First and Second *Critiques*," *Southwest Philosophical Studies* (Spring 1978), pp. 51–58.

21. Patricia Kitcher, "Kant's Real Self," in *Self and Nature in Kant's Philosophy*, ed. Allen Wood (Ithaca, N. Y.: Cornell Univ. Press, 1984), pp. 113–47.

22. I hope the reader grasps this point. We separated, for a theoretical examination, two aspects of the argument in the Transcendental Deduction. Such a separation could be misleading, precisely because the argument is supposed to articulate the underlying unity that makes experience possible. The arguments are inextricably connected.

23. Kitcher, "Kant's Real Self," pp. 114–17.

24. Ibid., p. 114.

25. Hume, *Treatise*, ed. Selby-Bigge, p. 187.

26. John Locke, *An Essay Concerning Human Understanding*, ed. B. Rand (Cambridge: Harvard Univ. Press, 1931), iv, ix, 3.

27. In the note at B Preface, x1, Kant makes clear his concern. Harmless as idealism may seem, it is a scandal to philosophy and to human reason that the existence of things outside us must be accepted merely on faith. Kant's "Refutation of Idealism" attempts to rectify the situation by showing that the experience of self-consciousness, the requirement for any experience whatsoever, is possible only on the supposition of there being external objects. Thus, Kant's critique of Descartes amounts to the amusing claim that if Descartes were right, he must be wrong! If Descartes were right about the method of doubting everything external, as a means to arrive at an indubitable self-consciousness, he would never have discovered anything. for the self is not a substance, and if one removes all outer objects, one would never have the experience of self-consciousness.

28. Kant, *Critique*, A182/B224–A189/B232.

29. Special thanks also to Darrel Johnson, Stephen Kennett, and Stephen W. Smith for their editorial assistance.

ROBERT HAHN IS ASSOCIATE PROFESSOR, DEPARTMENT OF PHILOSOPHY, Southern Illinois University at Carbondale. He received his Ph.D. degree from Yale University and has previously taught at Yale University; the University of Texas, Arlington; Brandeis; Harvard; and Denison universities; as well as at The American College of Greece, Athens. His journal articles have appeared in *Apeiron, The Journal of Chinese Philosophy, Journal of the History of Philosophy, Philosophical Research Archives, Phronesis, The Southwest Journal of Philosophy,* and *Southwest Philosophical Studies*.